MEN
ON
RAPE

MEN ON RAPE

Timothy Beneke

St. Martin's Press
New York

The author gratefully acknowledges permission to reprint two lines from "Legend" from *The Complete Poems and Selected Letters and Prose of Hart Crane,* edited by Brom Weber, with the permission of Liveright Publishing Corporation, copyright 1933, © 1958, 1966 by Liveright Publishing Corporation.

Library of Congress Cataloging in Publication Data

Beneke, Timothy.
  Men on rape

  1. Rape—United States—Public opinion.
2. Public opinion—United States. 3. Men—
United States—Attitudes. 4. Men—United States—
Interviews. I. Title.
HV6561.B46   364.1′532′0973   82–5628
ISBN 0–312–52950–3   AACR2
ISBN 0-312-52951-1 PBK.

For Dad

Contents

Acknowledgments

Kathie Jacobson was an inspiration; much of what I have come to understand about violence against women can be traced to her. Allan Creighton was a friend, scrupulous conscience, and out-of-house editor for much of the book. I was awfully lucky to have had many extraordinary discussions with George Lakoff in which I learned a great deal about language, the world, and issues relating to men, women, and rape. His influence is strongly felt in the introduction (though he may not agree with everything I say).

My discussions with Sue Bessmer gave me confidence and insight. Rich Snowdon always had perceptive and wise things to say. Erving Goffman was kind enough to let me develop a distinction he made in conversation. Jack Painter and postural integration kept me relaxed, energized, and clear. James McMullen offered me kindnesses for which I am immensely grateful. Marcia Markland, my initial editor at St. Martin's, was a source of strength and enthusiasm. Ashton Applewhite, my final editor, did a perceptive and thorough editing job. Laura X and the National Clearinghouse on Marital Rape (Berkeley, California) helped open my eyes on marital rape issues.

And so many other people who believed in the project and shared their perspectives with me! Among them I would like to thank Bob Heaton, Sally Werson, Camille Le Grand, Naomi Quinn, Mark Johnson, Barbara Dixson, Charlotte Linde, Jane

Creighton, Jim Ruttenbur, Andrea Rechtin, Cassandra Sagan, Katy Riker, Marvin Lehrman, Steven Heath, Claire Risley, Leslie Bennis, Christopher Hewitt, Sam Julty, Ben Goldberg, Evie Roberts, Tim Nesbitt, Robin Skidmore-McNight, Star, Slava Ellis, Clark Craig, Paula Camacho, Kate Raisz, Lesli Josephson, and Barry Shapiro.

I wish to further acknowledge an intellectual debt to Susan Brownmiller, Diana Russell, and Susan Griffin whose groundbreaking works made this book possible.

In addition, I would like to thank my agent, Howard Buck, and finally, all of the men who were willing to talk with me about rape in the presence of a tape recorder; both those whose words found their way into the book and those whose didn't.

Timothy Beneke

Berkeley, California

Preface

This book in no way aspires to be "objective" or "scientific"; I did not set out to draw definite conclusions about what men as a group think or feel about rape. Rather I set out to explore and map a significant portion of the territory that constitutes men's consciousness of rape, and to think hard about the assumptions that supported the consciousness I found. The introduction in large measure examines and analyzes a few of those assumptions.

I cannot say to what extent the interviews accurately represent the attitudes of men in American culture; I can say that they accurately represent the attitudes *presented* by the men who were willing to talk; I am certain they cover a considerable part of the spectrum. Taken as a whole, these men are probably a bit younger, more articulate, and more middle-class than the average. I was less concerned with presenting balance in age, class, or race than with exploring and revealing salient feelings, attitudes, and perceptions.

Another point: this book is about the rape of women. I wanted to interview a man who had been raped, but was unable to find a man who would consent to an interview. That fact alone may say more than the interview would have. For what it's worth, men also rape other men, most commonly (though by no means exclusively) in prisons, jails, and reformatories. At its source if not in its effect, the issue is the same as in the rape of women: male sexual violence.

A final note. In the introduction I alternately refer to women who have been raped as rape *victims* and rape *survivors*. Both terms strike me as having merit. It is important to bring the concept of *rape survivors* into our vocabulary, for it speaks to the reality of rape as an experience that calls a woman's very survival into question.

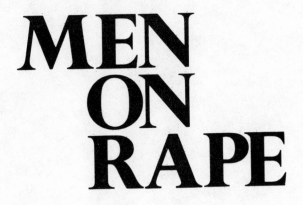

MEN
ON
RAPE

I

Introduction

Rape and Constraint

Rape may be America's fastest growing violent crime; no one can be certain because it is not clear whether more rapes are being committed or reported. It *is* clear that violence against women is widespread and fundamentally alters the meaning of life for women; that sexual violence is encouraged in a variety of ways in American culture; and that women are often blamed for rape.

Consider some statistics:

• In a random sample of 930 women, sociologist Diana Russell found that 44 percent had survived either rape or attempted rape. Rape was defined as sexual intercourse physically forced upon the woman, or coerced by threat of bodily harm, or forced upon the woman when she was helpless (asleep, for example). The survey included rape and attempted rape in marriage in its calculations. (Personal communication)

• In a September 1980 survey conducted by *Cosmopolitan* magazine to which over 106,000 women anonymously responded, 24 percent had been raped at least once. Of those, 51 percent had been raped by friends, 37 percent by strangers, 18 percent by relatives, and 3 percent by husbands. 10 percent of the women in the survey had been victims of incest. 75 percent of the women had been "bullied into making love." Writer Linda Wolfe, who reported on the survey, wrote in reference to such bullying: "Though such harassment stops short of rape, readers reported that it was nearly as distressing."

• An estimated 2–3 percent of all men who rape outside of marriage go to prison for their crimes.[1]

• The F.B.I. estimates that if current trends continue, one woman in four will be sexually assaulted in her lifetime.[2]

• An estimated 1.8 million women are battered by their spouses each year.[3] In extensive interviews with 430 battered women, clinical psychologist Lenore Walker, author of *The Battered Woman,* found that 59.9 percent had also been raped (defined as above) by their spouses. Given the difficulties many women had in admitting they had been raped, Walker estimates the figure may well be as high as 80 or 85 percent. (Personal communication.) If 59.9 percent of the 1.8 million women battered each year are also raped, then a million women may be raped in marriage each year. And a significant number are raped in marriage without being battered.

• Between one in two and one in ten of all rapes are reported to the police.[4]

• Between 300,000 and 500,000 women are raped each year outside of marriage.[5]

What is often missed when people contemplate statistics on rape is the effect of the *threat* of sexual violence on women. I have asked women repeatedly, "How would your life be different if rape were suddenly to end?" (Men may learn a lot by asking this question of women to whom they are close.) The threat of rape is an assault upon the meaning of the world; it alters the feel of the human condition. Surely any attempt to comprehend the lives of women that fails to take issues of violence against women into account is misguided.

Through talking to women, I learned: *The threat of rape alters the meaning and feel of the night.* Observe how your body feels, how the night feels, when you're in fear. The constriction in your chest, the vigilance in your eyes, the rubber in your legs. What do the stars look like? How does the moon present itself? What is the difference between walking late at night in the dangerous part of a city and walking late at night in the country, or safe suburbs? When I try to imagine what the threat of rape must do to the night, I think of the stalked, adrenalated feeling I get walking late at night in parts of certain American cities. Only, I remind myself, it is a fear different from any I have known, a fear of being raped.

It is night half the time. If the threat of rape alters the meaning of the night, it must alter the meaning and pace of the day, one's relation to the passing and organization of time itself. For some women, the threat of rape at night turns their cars into armored tanks, their solitude into isolation. And what must the space inside a car or an apartment feel like if the space outside is menacing?

I was running late one night with a close woman friend through a path in the woods on the outskirts of a small university town. We had run several miles and were feeling a warm, energized serenity.

"How would you feel if you were alone?" I asked.

"Terrified!" she said instantly.

"Terrified that there might be a man out there?" I asked, pointing to the surrounding moonlit forest, which had suddenly been transformed into a source of terror.

"Yes."

Another woman said, "I know what I can't do and I've completely internalized what I can't do. I've built a viable life that basically involves never leaving my apartment at night unless I'm directly going some place to meet somebody. It's unconsciously built into what it occurs to women to do." When one is raised without freedom, one may not recognize its absence.

The threat of rape alters the meaning and feel of nature. Everyone has felt the psychic nurturance of nature. Many women are being deprived of that nurturance, especially in wooded areas near cities. They are deprived either because they cannot experience nature in solitude because of threat, or because, when they do choose solitude in nature, they must cope with a certain subtle but nettlesome fear.

Women need more money because of rape and the threat of rape makes it harder for women to earn money. It's simple: if you don't feel safe walking at night, or riding public transportation, you need a car. And it is less practicable to live in cheaper, less secure, and thus more dangerous neighborhoods if the ordinary threat of violence that men experience, being mugged, say, is compounded by the threat of rape. By limiting mobility at night, the threat of rape limits where and when one is able to work, thus making it more difficult to earn money. An obvious bind: women need more money because of rape, and have fewer job opportunities because of it.

The threat of rape makes women more dependent on men (or other women). One woman said: "If there were no rape I wouldn't have to play games with men for their protection." The threat of rape falsifies, mystifies, and confuses relations between men and women. If there were no rape, women would simply not need men as much, wouldn't need them to go places with at night, to feel safe in their homes, for protection in nature.

The threat of rape makes solitude less possible for women. Solitude, drawing strength from being alone, is difficult if being alone means being afraid. To be afraid is to be in need, to experience a lack; the threat of rape creates a lack. Solitude requires relaxation; if you're afraid, you can't relax.

The threat of rape inhibits a woman's expressiveness. "If there were no rape," said one woman, "I could dress the way I wanted and walk the way I wanted and not feel self-conscious about the responses of men. I could be friendly to people. I wouldn't have to wish I was ugly. I wouldn't have to make myself small when I got on the bus. I wouldn't have to respond to verbal abuse from men by remaining silent. I could respond in kind."

If a woman's basic expressiveness is inhibited, her sexuality, creativity, and delight in life must surely be diminished.

The threat of rape inhibits the freedom of the eye. I know a married couple who live in Manhattan. They are both artists, both acutely sensitive and responsive to the visual world. When they walk separately in the city, he has more freedom to look than she does. She must control her eye movements lest they inadvertently meet the glare of some importunate man. What, who, and how she sees are restricted by the threat of rape.

The following exercise is recommended for men.

Walk down a city street. Pay a lot of attention to your clothing; make sure your pants are zipped, shirt tucked in, buttons done. Look straight ahead. Every time a man walks past you, avert your eyes and make your face expressionless. Most women learn to go through this act each time we leave our houses. It's a way to avoid at least some of the encounters we've all had with strange men who decided we looked available.[6]

To relate aesthetically to the visual world involves a certain playfulness, a spirit of spontaneous exploration. The tense vigilance that accompanies fear inhibits that spontaneity. The world is no longer yours to look at when you're afraid.

I am aware that all culture is, in part, restriction, that there are places in America where hardly anyone is safe (though men are safer than women virtually everywhere), that there are many ways to enjoy life, that some women may not be so restricted, that there exist havens, whether psychic, geographical, economic, or class. But they are *havens,* and as such, defined by threat.

Above all, I trust my experience: no woman could have lived the life I've lived the last few years. If suddenly I were restricted by the threat of rape, I would feel a deep, inexorable depression. And it's not just rape; it's harassment, battery, Peeping Toms, anonymous phone calls, exhibitionism, intrusive stares, fondlings— all contributing to an atmosphere of intimidation in women's lives. And I have only scratched the surface; it would take many carefully crafted short stories to begin to express what I have only hinted at in the last few pages. I have not even touched upon what it might mean for a woman to be sexually assaulted. Only women can speak to that (see Chapter 8). Nor have I suggested how the threat of rape affects marriage.

Rape and the threat of rape pervade the lives of women, as reflected in some popular images of our culture.

Rape Signs

"As silent as a mirror is believed
Realities plunge in silence by . . ."

Hart Crane
"Legends"

Close your eyes and imagine a caveman. What is he doing and to whom?

Most people see him clubbing a cavewoman (usually walking by herself) over the head and dragging her off by the hair. Most people *don't* see blood gushing from the cavewoman's head, scrapes and bruises accumulating on her legs as she's dragged over uncleared ground, her look of dazed horror when she's hit. And the scene in the cave? What happens there? Presumably he rapes her while she's un- (or semi-) conscious.

This scene, which lives in most of our minds, which has evoked wry laughter in most of us at one time or another (I remember its winsome presentation in cartoons) is a *rape sign*. A rape sign is a way of expressing ideas and feelings about rape without acknowledging them to ourselves. As we shall see, the caveman scene expresses many ideas and feelings related to rape, yet we ordinarily fail to notice that the scene is *about* rape. Rape signs are manifest in jokes, images, verbal expressions, songs, stories, etc. Rape can be humorized, eroticized, aestheticized, athleticized, and (usually) trivialized, without anyone realizing that rape has been referred to. Rape is made safe because we are allowed to express possibly dangerous feelings and thoughts while simultaneously discounting them. Rape signs mask a tenuous, anxiety-ridden relationship to rape.

We *need* rape signs. We *demand* them. The evidence is their ubiquity. Rape signs stand between us and the reality of rape, obfuscating and numbing our vision and sensitivity. They paralyze thought much in the way habit paralyzes spontaneity. They tell us false stories about rape, men, and women without our consciously hearing the stories.

Why is it, *how* is it that I saw the caveman scene for years and never connected it to rape? How is it that many of us have been laughing at rape for years without knowing it?

We can relate to the caveman scene in at least three ways. (1) We can contemplate what, in the very simplest sense, the scene expresses. (2) We can examine and analyze the ideas about men, women, our sexual selves, etc., which are expressed by the scene. Or, (3) we can experience the scene in the ambiguous half-conscious way most of us experience such phenomena; perhaps as droll, or trivial, or distracting—but nonetheless as something that insidiously teaches us about the world.[7]

Let us contemplate the scene in the simplest sense. A cavewoman is walking along. Is she thinking? Does she think in a way similar to the way we do? Is she afraid? Is she attuned to her senses in a way wholly different from the way we are? Is her universe full of friendly and unfriendly spirits? How does one begin to relate to her?

And the caveman. What is his mood? Why does he commit this vicious assault? It is painful to ponder the blood and bruises as he drags her away. Taken simply, this scene is quite horrible. Yet many of us miss the horror and half consciously "receive" a familiar set of ideas about men, women, sexuality, power, and our "natural" selves.

Let us look at some of the ideas suggested by the caveman scene. First, that rape is natural, that in some natural state, unfettered by civilization and its discontents, men would rape women, especially if women are walking by themselves. Since rape is natural, men are not ultimately responsible.

Second, that rape isn't rape. We see the image repeatedly and never connect it with rape. We laugh at it, we are overfamiliar with it. *Somehow* we deny that it's rape. Just as words like "passed away" or "powder room" serve to hide the realities of death and excretion, the caveman scene hides the reality of rape while simultaneously legitimizing it.

Third, that physical strength is a legitimate source of power in man/woman and other types of interaction. We see a *big* caveman and a *little* cavewoman. This idea of the legitimacy of physical strength as a source of power in relations between men and women is much more with us than is generally acknowledged. Superior male strength and the threat of violence provides a kind of background to relations between men and women. Its exploitation can be seen in men's raised voices in arguments, their catcalls, their body language, to say nothing of their actual physical violence against women.

Fourth, that women don't really suffer when they're attacked and raped. We don't see or hear her cry out; we don't see her struggle or resist; we don't see her blood. The reality of her experience is denied; we don't identify with her.

Fifth, that women are somehow supposed to be attracted to brute strength. Her lack of resistance, her lack of visible suffering suggest that she secretly wishes to be ravished by the (big, strong) man.

Sixth, the caveman's experience is legitimized. We are encouraged to identify with and admire him. He experiences a kind of triumph, what one might call the thrill of conquest.

Seventh, the scene implies that uncontrolled violent emotion and desire is "primitive" and rational control and decency are "civilized," something the "advanced" civilizations of the twentieth century scarcely confirm.

And we are in the habit of seeing the caveman scene without recognizing or examining these ideas, and without objecting to their destructive consequences as beliefs about men and women.

The notion that rape is "just human nature" and therefore cannot be stopped pervades our thought about rape. As one district attorney said, "You're not going to stop rape. Social rapes are always going to happen. I don't care if it's Adam and Eve, or Luke Skywalker and Princess Leah, it's always going to happen. That's just human nature." (See Chapter 5, Lawyers, "John.")

But rape is not just "human nature"; rape is *not* "natural." In her study of rape in tribal societies, anthropologist Peggy Reeves Sanday found that out of ninety-five tribal societies, 47 percent were rape free, 18 percent rape prone, and 35 percent somewhere in between. According to Sanday:

Rape in tribal societies is part of a cultural configuration which includes interpersonal violence, male dominance, and sexual separation. In such societies, as the Murphys say about the Mundurucu: "men . . . use the penis to dominate their women." The question remains as to what motivates the rape prone cultural configuration. Considerable evidence suggests that this configuration evolves in societies faced with depleting food resources, migration or other factors contributing to a dependence on male distribution capacities as opposed to female fertility.[8]

According to Sanday, when men are in harmony with their environment, rape is usually absent.

It's important to understand that violence is socially and not biologically programmed. Rape is not an integral part of male nature, but the means by which men programmed for violence express their social selves. Men who are conditioned to respect the female virtues of growth and the sacredness of life do not violate women. It is significant that in societies where nature is held sacred, rape occurs only rarely.[9]

Once we acknowledge that rape is not natural, we are forced to acknowledge that something has gone wrong in a culture such as ours where rape is common. Thinking of rape as natural can no longer be used to evade responsibility for it.

Cartoons in men's magazines provide another occasional source of rape signs. Such cartoons often portray a man chasing a woman, usually around a room. It may be a judge chasing a woman accused of a crime, a boss chasing his secretary, a patient chasing a nurse. Such cartoons clearly portray a man trying to force sex on a woman; they clearly suggest that such situations are funny. They exploit the widely held belief that if a man and a woman know each other, or if the man has no weapon, it's not really rape if the man forces sex upon the woman. Yet we seldom connect such cartoons to rape.

Rape signs pervade American culture. One can find them in pornography, advertising, song lyrics, album covers, novels, etc. And there is an important sense in which the rape fantasies of men (and probably women) constitute a kind of rape sign. In all of the sexual fantasies of rape that I have heard men recount, the experience as described by women, with its terror and fear of death, is denied. Just as rape signs make it difficult to think clearly about rape, men's fantasies of rape may make it difficult for men to think about the reality of rape.

Rape Language[10]

"fuck (taboo) vt. To cheat, trick, take advantage of, deceive or treat someone unfairly. Very common. The relationship between sex and fraud is best illustrated by this usage . . ."
Dictionary of American Slang
Compiled by Harold Wentworth and Stuart Berg Flexner.

Two apparently conflicting statements are often made about rape. First, that rape is a crime of violence and has little to do with sex. And second, that rape is merely an extension of the sex roles and sexual behavior regularly played out between men and women. In discussing this, we must distinguish the experience of the victim from that of the rapist.

It is clear that the experience of being raped for a woman has plenty to do with violence and terror, and little to do with sex. And it is important to get people to understand rape not in terms of sex, but as brutal physical and psychic violence. And it appears to be true that rapists (at least the ones who end up incarcerated and studied) are seldom trying to meet "sexual needs" when they rape.

But what exactly is a sexual need? And what distinguishes sexual from nonsexual needs? Are "ordinary men" when they seek to have sex with women trying to meet sexual needs? Are there any similarities between "ordinary men" and rapists when they have sex?

One way to answer such a question is by analyzing the way men talk about sex and women. George Lakoff and Mark Johnson, in a remarkable book, *Metaphors We Live By,*[11] acutely discern many fundamental metaphorical concepts by which we conceive of, live in, and experience the world. In a metaphor, we understand and experience one kind of thing in terms of another. According to Lakoff and Johnson, most of the way we understand and structure our experience is metaphorical. A *metaphorical concept* is a way in which we *repeatedly* understand and structure our experience that is manifested in the way we speak. To illustrate:

TIME IS MONEY: You've got to learn to *budget* your time. That *cost* me a lot of time. He's living on *borrowed* time. This gadget will *save* you hours. That's a stupid way to *spend* your time.

"Time Is Money" functions as a metaphorical concept structuring our experience of and relationship to time. According to Lakoff and Johnson:

Metaphors may create realities for us, especially social realities. A metaphor may thus be a guide for future action. Such actions will, of course, fit the metaphor. This will in turn reinforce the power of the metaphor to make experience coherent. In this sense metaphors can be self-fulfilling prophecies.[12]

How do men metaphorically structure their experience when they wish to have sex consensually with a woman, or when they have just had sex consensually with a woman? How do they understand what they have done, would like to do, or are going to do? One theme, particularly common to younger men who are seeking an initial sexual encounter with a woman, goes like this: having sex is an achievement; the achievement is gaining possession of a valued commodity; the valued commodity is a woman. Men who are relating to women in this way will tend, when they speak, to focus either on sex as achievement or the woman as a commodity.

Sex as achievement is often expressed in simple, straightforward ways.

SEX IS ACHIEVEMENT: I'd like to *make it* with her. Maybe I'll *get her into bed.* You didn't have to *work very hard* to *get into her pants.*

The achievement can also be expressed as a successful hunt or conquest, as doing well in a game, as winning a gambling game, as winning a war, or as getting a woman to provide sexual servicing:

SEX IS A HUNT, A CONQUEST: I'm going *to go out and get a piece of ass* tonight.

SEX IS A GAME: I hope I *score* tonight. I *struck out* with her.

SEX IS A GAMBLING GAME: If you *play your cards right,* you'll score. Your *best bet* is not to come on too strong.

SEX IS WAR: I tried to get her into bed but *got shot down.* If I can *wear down her resistance,* I'll score. He's always *hitting on* women.

SEX IS BEING SERVICED BY A WOMAN: She wouldn't *put out for me.* She *did it for him* but she wouldn't *do it for me.*

After the man has succeeded in gaining the woman's consent, sex is still achievement. Only now the achievement is performing well sexually.

SEX IS PERFORMANCE: You were *great last night.* I wasn't able to *fill the bill* sexually with her. I got *rave reviews* in bed. He's *good in bed.*

And one's performance may be understood as instruction, triumph, or triumph through inflicting pleasure.

SEX IS INSTRUCTION: I know how to *show a woman a good time.* A man needs to be in good shape when he *takes a woman to bed.* You could *learn a lot* from me, baby. I could *teach her a thing or two.*

SEX IS TRIUMPH: I really *put it to her!* I really *stuck it to her!*

SEX IS TRIUMPH THROUGH INFLICTING PLEASURE: Boy, did I *make her moan!* I *got her so hot* she could hardly stand it!

When the emphasis is on the woman as a valued commodity she is taken to be an object, sometimes food, that can be possessed or stolen.

SEX IS A COMMODITY: I've never had to *pay for pussy.* Why should a man rape if he can *get it for free?* She wouldn't *give me any.* I've been *getting it regularly* lately. Do you know any *available* women?

SEX IS POSSESSION: I'd like to *have her* for a night. I bet I could *get her* if I tried. You're *gonna lose* that girl.

SEX IS THEFT: She's good *snatch*. If she won't give it, I'm going to *take it*. He's *robbing the cradle*. I'd like to *cop some ass*.

SEX IS FOOD: She was the *best piece of ass* I ever had. What a *dish!*

WOMEN ARE OBJECTS: She's a cute *thing*. Take off your clothes and show me your *stuff*. Check *that* out. How would you like a *little bit of that?* She likes to *flaunt it*.

Men may think of women as animals, children, or their genitals.

WOMEN ARE ANIMALS: She's a nice *chick*. Wow, check out the *pet* of the month. She works as a Playboy *bunny*. She's real *foxy*. Let's see if we can shoot some *squirrel* (or *beaver*). She's really a *dog*. What a *bitch!*

WOMEN ARE CHILDREN: Do you like the *girls* at the office? Janice is our *playmate* of the month! Hey, *baby!*

WOMEN ARE THEIR GENITALS: She's a *cunt*.

Sexual feeling may be seen as being out of one's control. This notion pervades much of our talk about sex.

SEX IS MADNESS: I'm *wild* with desire. Every time I look at a woman *I go crazy*.

SEXUAL FEELING IS ELECTRICITY/FLUIDS CONTROLLED BY A WOMAN: She *turns me on*. She really *got my juices flowing*. One look at her and I'm all *stirred up*.

If sexual feeling is out of one's control, it is not surprising that sex itself may be understood as violence.

SEX IS HITTING A WOMAN'S GENITALS: I'd like to *bang* her *box*.

MASTURBATION IS HITTING ONE'S OWN GENITALS: I *beat my meat* last night. I like to *whack off*.

IMPREGNATION IS AN ACT OF VIOLENCE: He *knocked her up*.

A PENIS IS A GUN; SPERM IS AMMUNITION: He *shot his load* into her.

The above examples partially illustrate how a significant number of heterosexual men structure their experience of themselves, women, and sex. Most heterosexual men have used some of the above phrases at one time or another, and some men regularly talk this way. What characterizes men's activity when they regard sex as an achievement, and the achievement as gaining possession of a valued commodity, and the valued commodity is a woman? I will address four basic aspects: *status, hostility, control,* and *dominance.*

Status. Clearly, achievement has much to do with status. Performing, triumphing, instructing, winning wars, conquering, and being serviced are all activities that confer superior status. And gaining possession of a valued commodity also gives one status in two ways: one has status over the woman because one possesses her, and one is given status in the eyes of other men.

Hostility. To regard women as commodities to possess is an act of hostility. To regard women as objects, animals, food, or children is also, as is thinking of sex as war, triumph, theft, hitting a woman's genitals, a hunt, or possession.

Control. In achieving possession of a commodity, one is trying to maintain control, to control the woman's behavior and control one's own performance.

Dominance. To possess a commodity is to dominate it; to triumph, win a war, succeed in a hunt, win a game, or be serviced by a woman all express dominance.

It would appear that for many men seeking sex with a woman, sex has more to do with the above than with sensual pleasure or sexual satisfaction. Is there a similarity between what such men are concerned with when they have sex with a woman and what rapists are concerned with?

Status, hostility, control, and dominance. I first found these features mentioned in clinical psychologist Nicholas Groth's discussion of rapists. Based upon careful clinical study of over five hundred sex offenders, Groth concluded:

Rape, then, is a pseudosexual act, a pattern of sexual behavior that is concerned much more with *status, hostility, control,* and *dominance* than with sensual pleasure or sexual satisfaction. It is sexual behavior in the primary service of non-sexual needs.[13] (Italics mine.)

Not every man is a rapist, but every man who grows up in America and learns American English learns all too much to think like a rapist, to structure his experience of women and sex in terms of status, hostility, control, and dominance. If we are going to say that, for a man, rape has little to do with sex, we may as well add that sex itself often has little to do with sex, or, if you like, that rape has plenty to do with sex as it is often understood and spoken about by men.

Contrary to the impression one might get from reading newspapers, much rape appears to be between acquaintances, often on dates. If men go out on dates with the idea that sex is achievement of possession of a valued commodity, the woman's consent is likely to be of peripheral concern.

I am unaware of any felicitious way of talking about sex in American English. One can speak of wanting to go to bed with, sleep with, or make love with a woman. It is as if to speak in a somewhat human, sharing way about sexual desire requires that the funky, lusty side of sex be denied. I am not aware of any common English phrases that allow one to express sexual desire in a way that acknowledges both lust and humanity. And at any rate, men speak the way they do regarding sex in part because of the way they feel and because of what their language and culture provide. And being repulsed by most of the language available to talk about sex and learning to speak a different language doesn't mean that one's gut feelings about sex or women change.

Consider five more or less familiar statements:

Fuck you!
I got screwed by the I.R.S.
Get fucked!

He's a real mind fuck!
Fuck it!

These statements reflect a common folk theory of sex.[14] A folk theory is a commonsense model of some aspect of reality. In a metaphor we understand one thing in terms of another; in a folk theory two normally separate things may be so collapsed together that it is difficult to separate them. We are able to make sense of the above statements because we not only understand sex in terms of aggression and degradation, but because we actually take sex to *be* that.

SEX IS AGGRESSIVE DEGRADATION: I'd like to *screw* her. I want to *fuck* her.

And if sex is aggression or degradation, a penis is a weapon. "Fuck you!" and "Get fucked!" are both rape insults. In an insult one often verbally wishes on someone what one would like to see happen physically. "I got screwed," expresses a feeling of violation; "Fuck it" a desire to dominate and abuse (through sexual means). Someone mind-fucking you is abusing your mind and treating it disrespectfully.

Try saying "Fuck you!" aloud several times. What thoughts, feelings, or images arise? Is there anyone you wish to say this to? In wishing to say this, are you wishing violation and rape upon them? A rapist who uses his penis as a weapon is acting out a value that we express regularly. A man may never relate to women in a sexually abusive way, but if he uses this language he is reflecting a view of sex as an aggressive, degrading act.

"Fuck" (in its narrowly sexual sense) doesn't always signify aggressive degradation of one person by another. "Let's fuck" expresses both lust and mutuality (of a sort). Tone of voice and context can give "fuck" many different connotations, but there is usually a sense of dirt and degradation attached to it.

When we say "Fuck you!" etc., we are expressing anger and frustration. But in calmer moments we agree that it is wrong and undesirable to fuck someone over, or to "screw" someone. We don't, for the most part, say with pride: "I really fucked him over!"

But there does exist a set of phrases men use where forced aggression, a kind of symbolic rape, is considered desirable and where men express pride and triumph in it.

WINNING IS FORCED AGGRESSION: Go out there and *stick it to them!* We really *put it to the Acme Corporation! Sock it* to them! Any time a situation exists which is sufficiently competitive to be thought of as a war (athletic events, competition in business, intellectually competing schools in academia) the sentiment may arise that we must stick it (put it, sock it) to them before they stick it to us.[15]

This language may well have the unconscious effect of intimidating women. If the fear of rape (or avoiding situations that may evoke the fear of rape) is a significant part of a woman's life, then what is the effect of hearing all this rape language? Suppose a woman has been sexually assaulted. What is the effect, however unconscious, of hearing expressions that imply a cultural view of sex as aggression or degradation? (That some women themselves use this language is no indication that it doesn't intimidate. One can be intimidated by one's own language.)

This language probably will not change till our conception of sex changes. For the present, it is important to know what we're saying and why we're saying it.

We have analyzed some of the ways men conceive of sex: now we will look at some of the ways they view rape.

First, when men speak sympathetically about women's experiences of being raped, they conceive of it as a violent intrusion; the violent intrusion can be either a cut or an invasion of sacred space. (Women often conceive of rape in this way as well.)

RAPE IS A PHYSICAL WOUND, PROBABLY A CUT: One speaks of a *sexual trauma.* Rape is often referred to as a *wound* that takes time *to heal* and leaves a *scar.* (See Chapter 6, Doctors, "Herb.") This is not generally thought of as a metaphor, since the idea of a psychic trauma is itself not thought of as a metaphor. This metaphor appears to cohere with many of the processes women go through after they've been raped.

RAPE IS INVASION OF SACRED SPACE: Many people speak of rape as the violation of the most private, sacred part of a person. This suggests that the vagina is a private, sacred space and, perhaps, that sex is a religious experience. (See Chapter 4, Husbands, Lovers, Friends, "Gary.")

When men identify with the rapist they often speak of rape as theft, instruction, defilement, revenge, and "natural."

RAPE IS THEFT OF A VALUED COMMODITY: Men often speak of rape as "going out and taking it." "Why should a man rape if he can get it for free?" suggests one man. (See Chapter 2, A Variety of Men, "Hank.") If a man understands sex as a commodity, then rape may be seen as theft of the commodity. This view is reflected in the absence of marital rape laws in all but a few states: a man can't steal what he already owns.

RAPE IS INSTRUCTION: Rapists sometimes say to their victims, "I'll show you what life is about." (See Chapter 8, An Advocate for Rape Victims Responds.) And men who think sex is instruction have been known to say things like: "Rape isn't so bad. He's only trying to show her a good time."

RAPE IS DEFILEMENT OF PROPERTY: This view is reflected in the notion that one can't rape a prostitute because one can't defile already defiled goods. And some relationships between men and women break up because the man no longer regards the woman as "pure"; he sees her as dirtied or spoiled or cheapened. It is as if her vagina is clean, valued property and rape dirties it.

RAPE IS REVENGE: When they examine their own rape fantasies some men find their origin in revenge. Some men feel that women have enormous power in their appearance and that rape is getting even. (See Chapter 2, A Variety of Men, "Jay," "Joe.") And Chuck (see Chapter 3, Rapist) speaks of rape as getting back at women who'd hurt him in the past.

RAPE IS NATURAL, BOYS BEING BOYS: As has already been elaborated, there is nothing "natural" about rape.

What is taken by men to be the woman's weapon? Consider a few more expressions.

She's a *knockout!*
What a *bombshell!*
She's *strikingly* beautiful!
That woman is *ravishing!*
She's really *stunning!*
She's a *femme fatale!*
She's *dressed to kill!*

Clearly to men, a woman's *appearance* is a weapon.[16] It can knock a man out, explode and kill him, strike him, it can ravish him (notice the reversal—*she* rapes *him* with her appearance), it can stun, i.e., hit him on the head and again (twice) it can kill him. Everyone, man or woman, who learns American English and can understand the seven sentences above at least unconsciously understands a woman's appearance as a powerful physical force.

Most heterosexual men have felt this. This power is due not so much to anything physiological (though that must play a role) but more to the ways men understand sex. If sex is achievement, then the presence of an attractive woman may result in one's feeling like a failure. One's self worth, or "manhood" may become subtly (or not so subtly) at issue in her presence. And how does one feel toward someone who "makes one feel like a failure"? Like degrading them in return. As long as sex is achievement ("I want to *make it* with her"), it will probably also be aggressive degradation ("I want to *fuck* her").

Explains "Jay" in Chapter 2:

Let's say I see a woman and she looks really pretty and really clean and sexy, and she's giving off very feminine, sexy vibes. I think, "Wow, I would love to make love to her," but I know she's not really interested. It's a tease. A lot of times a woman knows that she's looking really good and she'll use that and flaunt it, and it makes me feel like she's laughing at me and I feel *degraded.* I also feel dehumanized, because when I'm being teased I just turn off, I cease to be human. Because if I go with my human emotions I'm going to want to put my arms around her and kiss her, and to do that would be unacceptable. I don't like the feeling that I'm supposed to stand there and take it, and not be able to hug her or kiss her; so I just turn off my emotions. It's a feeling of humiliation, because the woman has forced me to turn off my feelings and react in a way that I really don't want to. If I were actually desperate enough to rape somebody, it would be from wanting the person, but also it would be a very spiteful thing, just being able to say, "I have power over you and I can do anything I want with you," because really I feel that *they* have power over *me* just by their presence. Just the fact that they can come up to me and just melt me and make me feel like a dummy makes me want revenge. They have power over me so I want power over them.

He feels degraded, he experiences humiliation in the presence of an attractive woman. So he wants to humiliate and degrade in return. Since sex is achievement, he feels like a failure around attractive women; he feels humiliated and degraded and wants to aggressively degrade back.

Notice the effect of women's appearances on him. Women are "giving off very feminine, sexy vibes"; he has "to stand there and take it"; he says that "the woman has forced me to turn off my feelings and react"; he claims that they have power over him "just by their presence"; they can come up to him and just "melt" him. A woman's appearance forces him to have sexual feelings he can't act upon; since he finds it unpleasant not to be able to act upon his sexual feelings, he must turn them off. It is, in part, an issue of potency. Women as he experiences them force him to feel sexually excited and then force him to turn off his excitement. They arouse and castrate him. His desire to get even constitutes a desire to reclaim potency.

Concepts like sexual *attraction,* which blur the distinction between sexual feeling and sexual action, are potentially danger-ous. The notion of sexual attraction is a metaphor derived from the natural sciences where two bodies are attracted to each other through magnetic, gravitational, or some other force. If having sexual feeling also means moving toward someone then at times when such movement is inappropriate, one must either repress sexual feelings or behave inappropriately. Neither solution works. If men can enjoy sexual feeling without needing to act upon it or be moved by it, they will feel less anger toward women and will be less likely to act out their anger.

Most heterosexual men have probably felt some of Jay's anger and frustration at one time or another. For many men, the predominant mood of adolescence is humiliation (or at least flight from humiliation through achievement); some of it is sexual humiliation, feeling inundated and barraged by images of women, whether from images in their own experience, the media, or their own psyches. Many men come to resent the power of these images and their own sexuality as well. One understanding of the penis as weapon: a means of getting even by inflicting pleasure (sex is triumph) and at least momentarily silencing the power of women's appearance, the power of women as images.

Growing up, I was thrown willy-nilly into a virtual manic-depressive oscillation between triumph and humiliation. The point of competition was to win, to triumph at someone else's expense. In sports, the idea was to humiliate one's opponent, to beat him (winning is battery), to stick it to him (winning is forced aggression). The situation was no different in the classroom; intellectual argument was war ("I *demolished* his argument") and one was supposed to win the war and demonstrate the stupidity of one's opponent. Feeling humiliated by women must be seen as a part of this larger humiliation; it must also be seen that this humiliation has little to do with women and much to do with absurd conceptions of masculinity.

Conceptions of sexual interaction that picture men as active and women as passive may ring false for many men, in part because they experience the woman's appearance as acting upon them. Looking at a man and a woman on a date from a third-person perspective, one may think that the man appears aggressive and the woman passive; the man and woman may experience themselves as equally acted upon, equally passive.

The idea that a woman's appearance is a weapon is inseparable from the notion that sexual pleasure makes one helpless. This idea pervades American culture, from the familiar Hollywood scene in which the heroine resists the kisses of the hero till, at a crucial moment, her resistance turns to the heavy breathing of sexual arousal and pleasure, to the stereotypical (and largely nonexistent) rapist who is said to have lost control at the sight of an attractive woman.

The appearance-as-weapon theme is used to justify rape and to justify insensitivity to women who have been raped. Part of the mentality goes: I cannot be sympathetic to people who have power over me and abuse that power; women have power over me and abuse that power in the way they dress, therefore I will not be sympathetic to women who are raped while they're abusing their power, i.e., who dress to look attractive.

George Lakoff (in conversation) has pointed out that the appearance-as-weapon theme is part of a more general passive theory of perception. Perception is understood in terms of external stimuli bombarding the senses—something that happens to me, over which I have no choice. We know that this is not true, that human beings actively perceive and make choices, whether conscious or unconscious, about what they perceive. Men often choose to perceive women's bodies in hidden, stolen ways, which brings us to our next section—pornographizing.

Pornographizing

Much has been written about pornography and rape. I would like to discuss *pornographizing* and rape. Pornographizing is important if we are to understand: (1) a bit more of most heterosexual men's consciousness of women; (2) pornography as an extension of that consciousness; and (3) how policemen, lawyers, doctors, and other men sometimes "re-rape" rape victims.

Pornographizing: the process by which men relate to women, images of women, the visual presence of women, stories about women, women in any way as PORNEA, which is Greek for "low whore."[17] How does one relate to a low whore? As property one uses for "sexual" pleasure. In pornographizing, one anonymises the woman and fails to acknowledge her moral, spiritual, or emotional being. One relates to her as a thing without soul. The woman as a locus of experience is denied. And often, one relates to her body as a fetish. A fetish: the new pair of shoes you stare and stare at that won't quite give you what you want. The new watch that shines in the dark but somehow leaves you empty. The thighs, breasts, calves, rears of women searched for throughout your adolescence. Images savored and extorted for lust. Pornographizing is the perceptual counterpart to sex as achievement of possession of a commodity and sex as aggressive degradation.

A connection exists between (1) men's repression of sexual (and other) feelings; (2) men's obsession with images of women as a kind of substitute for sexual feeling (the more one loses touch with sexual feeling, the more one needs images as a substitute) and (3) the brutalization of women. If sexual feeling is repressed and therefore sex is regarded as dirtying and evil, men may need to become obsessed with images of women's bodies to feel sexual. Those images may be regarded as evil and dirty. Women who are sexual may be so regarded. And since sexual women are dirty and evil (so goes the mentality), they deserve to be brutalized.

To the extent that one is obsessed with images, one relates to women as visual surfaces from which one can extort lust. Sexual feeling somehow begins to inhere in images of women, and women are given a strange, mystifying power. The intensity of one's orgasm may become connected to the intensity of the images one can evoke. The humanity of women can get lost in this process. Attractive women may come to signify undifferentiated lust. The woman's desire and the man's desire may become inseparable in the man's consciousness.

Sociologist Erving Goffman (in conversation) distinguishes two socially defined views of women's bodies: a stolen and an authorized view. An example of a stolen view would be a man stealing glances of women's breasts, thighs, etc., in a social situation. An example of an authorized view would be the Venus de Milo or any nude statute of a woman. And if a man stares lustfully at the crotch of the Venus de Milo? Then it becomes a stolen view.

I believe that there also exist authorized stolen views, stolen hearings, askings, touchings, and that stolen glances can at times be seen as *stealing visual property.* Let us look more closely at these distinctions.

AUTHORIZED VIEWS That a view is authorized confers no moral legitimacy upon it, though one reason views are unauthorized is because they're dehumanizing. Consider several authorized views of women's bodies.

A male art student in an art class drawing a nude woman model. He is authorized to look at her body in an attempt to faithfully render visual detail. If he looks out of a desire to excite lust in himself, his view is stolen. It is not *what* but *how* he sees that makes his view stolen.

Judges judging a bathing beauty contest are objectifying but not pornographizing women, at least in their capacity as judges. Their presumed concern is with proportion, grace of movement, etc. They are grading women's bodies. Again, if they see in a lustful way, their view becomes stolen.

A loving, nonsexist man looking lustfully at his wife. He experiences lust for her body while at the same time recognizing it as *her* body. It is simultaneously lust for her body or lust for her. He does not anonymize her.

One woman said to me: "I don't care how my lover looks at me as long as he knows that it's me. I broke up with a guy once because I didn't like the way he looked at me." If a man looks at his wife and blanks out her personality and just relates to her sexually as an anonymous body, then his view is stolen and pornographized. (Views can be stolen yet not pornographized, as we shall see.) He is relating to her as sexual property. This can be done in a spirit of play or sexual exploration (a form of authorized stealing) and be desirable. When done without clarity or honesty, it tends to be alienating.

STOLEN VIEWS   The prototypical stolen view is a man in a social situation stealing glances of women's bodies. This process is so fundamental a visual reflex in many men that they don't know they are doing it. If a man steals and retains an image of a woman and later uses it to enhance his orgasm he is in a sense stealing visual property. The image becomes his to use to give himself pleasure.

Consider a scene in a bar where a man is with his wife, whom he regards more or less as his property. Suppose another man looks lustfully at her. "What are you looking at?" says the husband. He regards his wife as his property; the man staring at her is stealing visual property that belongs to him. Only *he* is allowed to relate visually to her body in a sexual way. An unspoken element in his objection may have to do with his awareness that the man may steal her image.

Consider the notion of a Peeping Tom—he is essentially regarded as guilty of stealing visual property. And look at this entry from the *Dictionary of American Slang.*

Free show—a look or glance, usually at a girl's or woman's thighs or breasts, or occasionally at a nude woman, most often without the female's knowledge or consent, as when a girl or woman crosses her legs, or inadvertently forgets to close a door while disrobing. Mainly boy or young teenager use.[18]

Clearly, boys and young teenagers learn to regard a woman's body as valued visual property, which they can at times get to enjoy for free. In the conception of sex as a commodity, sex is something a man can buy, sell, get for free, or steal (rape). Similarly, a woman as visual property can be treated as a commodity to be bought, sold, gotten for free, or stolen.

No one should feel guilty about any sexual thoughts or feelings or fantasies they may have (though it is important to understand the meaning of such phenomena). Ideally, sexual feeling should make life delightful. Lust may intrude its ambivalent presence in many situations. Stealing glances of women's bodies need not be pornographizing. One can peripherally notice a woman's attractiveness without denying her humanity. A young boy may seek out glimpses of women's bodies with a certain wondrous sexual curiosity; it is only when he is properly socialized that he may learn to relate to women as less than human.

When stealing glances becomes disrespectful and intrusive, when it makes women uncomfortable, it becomes one end of a continuum that includes (among other things) catcalls, street and office harassment, battery, and rape.

The activity of relating to women as property in any form is oppressive; relating to women as visual property is significant because it is so seldom clearly acknowledged. Visual property has a kind of psychic primacy in men's relation to women as property. It is, I think, the first way that a boy learns to speak of a woman as property. And there exists an unpleasant psychic parallel between a man scanning his environment for visual property to steal and a rapist scanning his for women to rape.

AUTHORIZED STOLEN VIEWS   In American culture, authorized stealing is taken to be a source of pleasure. Forbidden fruit that one is authorized to eat tastes best. Look at a *Playboy* centerfold. Everything in the framing of the image and the image itself authorizes one to blank out the woman as a locus of experience and steal her image and appropriate it for pleasure.

Or a group of men harassing a woman as she walks by. They authorize each other to pornographize her, to relate to her as visual property, which they are unabashedly stealing.

Or a strip show. Men pay to enjoy visual property. A man deciding whether to hire a woman for a strip show is evaluating her as visual property.

Or the idea of a peep show. One pays to "peep," to steal an ostensibly illicit view.

SEMI-AUTHORIZED STOLEN VIEWS In singles' bars, where men and women dress with the understanding that they will "check each other out," apparently a certain semi-authorized stealing is allowed.

We can begin to relate these distinctions to what happens to a woman who's been raped.

If she goes to a doctor for an examination, he is authorized to view and touch her body. It is not what but how he sees and touches that determines whether he pornographizes her. He is technically authorized to make medical discriminations regarding the state of her body. If he pornographizes her and his body language, tone of voice, or comments reveal this, then he will have, in effect, re-raped the victim.

Just as there are authorized and stolen views, there are authorized and stolen askings and hearings. A policeman may be authorized to ask a rape victim questions he would otherwise never be authorized to ask a stranger—intimate, sexual (or pseudosexual) questions. If he and his fellow policemen are unethical or sexist, he may be authorized to pornographize in his questions and hearings. He may ask inappropriate questions; in effect treating the woman and her account of the rape as pornographic property. He may engage in no stolen asking but the way in which he hears may be stolen. Not *what,* but *how* he hears and how he relates to what he hears may constitute pornographizing. His comments or behavior may reveal his pornographizing. After reporting her rape to the police, one woman was told by the officer, "I don't want to be crude or nothing but your rapist sure knows how to pick 'em."

The same principle applies to the treatment of rape survivors by defense attorneys, prosecuting attorneys (see Chapter 5, Lawyers, "Robert" and "Bill"), and judges. A Denver judge, John Kane, was quoted as saying: "I just love to have a garden variety rape case. It keeps you awake in the afternoon and provides a little vicarious pleasure."[19] That he could even say this within earshot of the press and keep his job suggests that he feels (and is) authorized to pornographize rape survivors. Women sometimes speak of the "little rapes" that occur when they report the crime; the phrase strikes me as appropriate.

The ultimate pornographizing, the ultimate "stealing" is, of course, rape. Men are currently authorized to rape their wives in forty states. In many jurisdictions there exists a de facto authorization for men to rape women if they're on a date, if the woman is close friends with the man, if they have had sex before, or if they have consumed alcohol together. Anyone who pornographizes or mistreats a woman who's been raped is authorizing rape by making it harder for women to report the crime.

Stolen touchings is another category on a continuum with rape. There are plenty of jokes about "copping a feel—you can do a lot in a crowd." On subways, buses, and in other crowds, people are authorized to touch in inadvertent ways, but not to caress, poke, paw, etc. Most women who regularly spend time in crowds have stories to tell of stolen touchings.

Authorized touchings may be no better. Uncle Charlie may be socially authorized to hold his niece in his lap, but the way he holds her may constitute child molestation. His stolen touchings are another form of pornographizing.

What is it women often say about men stealing glances, hearings, touches from them? That they feel humiliated, cheapened, degraded, dehumanized. In short, they feel treated like *pornea,* low whores, and that is exactly what some men are doing to them. Other men, "good" men who tolerate this, collude in this brutalization.

I have discussed a number of ways we think about rape, sex, men, and women. Many of these ways result, as we shall see, in a further brutalization of women that is both cruel and insidious —blaming the rape victim.

"She Asked for It"—Blaming the Victim[20]

Many things may be happening when a man blames a woman for rape. We can now make a few points about what goes on when men (and some women) say, "She asked for it," (or are otherwise insensitive or dismissive) after a woman has been raped. (These points apply repeatedly to many of the interviews that follow.)

First, in all cases where a woman is said to have asked for it, her appearance and behavior are taken as a form of speech. "Actions speak louder than words" is a widely held belief; the woman's actions—her appearance may be taken as action—are given greater emphasis than her words; an interpretation alien to the woman's intentions is given to her actions. A logical extension of "she asked for it" is the idea that she wanted what happened to happen; if she wanted it to happen, she *deserved* for it to happen. Therefore, the man is not to be blamed. "She asked for it" can mean either that she was consenting to have sex and was not really raped, or that she was in fact raped but somehow she really deserved it. "If you ask for it, you deserve it," is a widely held notion. If I ask you to beat me up and you beat me up, I still don't deserve to be beaten up. So even if the notion that women asked to be raped had some basis in reality, which it doesn't, on its own terms it makes no sense.

Second, a mentality exists that says: a woman who assumes freedoms normally restricted to a man (like going out alone at night) and is raped is doing the same thing as a woman who goes out in the rain without an umbrella and catches a cold. Both are considered responsible for what happens to them. That men will rape is taken to be a legitimized given, part of nature, like rain or snow. The view reflects a massive abdication of responsibility for rape on the part of men. It is so much easier to think of rape as natural than to acknowledge one's part in it. So long as rape is regarded as natural, women will be blamed for rape.

A third point. The view that it is natural for men to rape is closely connected to the view of women as commodities. If a woman's body is regarded as a valued commodity by men, then of course, if you leave a valued commodity where it can be taken, it's just human nature for men to take it. If you left your stereo out on the sidewalk, you'd be asking for it to get stolen. Someone will just take it. (And how often men speak of rape as "going out and *taking it.*") If a woman walks the streets at night, she's leaving a valued commodity, her body, where it can be taken. So long as women are regarded as commodities, they will be blamed for rape.

Which brings us to a fourth point. "She asked for it" is inseparable from a more general "psychology of the dupe." If I use bad judgment and fail to read the small print in a contract and later get taken advantage of ("screwed" or "fucked over") then I deserve what I get; bad judgment makes me liable. Analogously, if a woman trusts a man and goes to his apartment, or accepts a ride hitchhiking, or goes out on a date and is raped, she's a dupe and deserves what she gets. "He didn't *really* rape her" goes the mentality—"he merely took advantage of her." And in America it's okay for people to take advantage of each other, even expected and praised. In fact, you're considered dumb and foolish if you don't take advantage of other people's bad judgment. And so, again, by treating them as dupes, rape will be blamed on women.

Fifth, if a woman who is raped is judged attractive by men, and particularly if she dresses to look attractive, then the mentality exists that she attacked him with her weapon so, of course, he counter-attacked with his. The preview to a popular movie states: "She was the victim of her own *provocative beauty.*" Provocation: "There is a line which, if crossed, will *set me off* and I will lose control and no longer be responsible for my behavior. If you punch me in the nose then, of course, I will not be responsible for what happens: you will have provoked a fight. If you dress, talk, move, or act a certain way, you will have provoked me to rape. If your appearance *stuns* me, *strikes* me, *ravishes* me, *knocks me out,* etc., then I will not be held responsible for what happens; you will have asked for it." The notion that sexual feeling makes one helpless is part of a cultural abdication of responsibility for sexuality. So long as a woman's appearance is viewed as a weapon and sexual feeling is believed to make one helpless, women will be blamed for rape.

Sixth, I have suggested that men sometimes become obsessed with images of women, that images become a substitute for sexual feeling, that sexual feeling becomes externalized and out of control and is given an undifferentiated identity in the appearance of women's bodies. It is a process of projection in which one blurs one's own desire with her imagined, projected desire. If a woman's attractiveness is taken to signify one's own lust and a woman's lust, then when an "attractive" woman is raped, some men may think she wanted sex. Since they perceive their own lust in part projected onto the woman, they disbelieve women who've been raped. So long as men project their own sexual desires onto women, they will blame women for rape.

And seventh, what are we to make of the contention that women in dating situations say "no" initially to sexual overtures from men as a kind of pose, only to give in later, thus revealing their true intentions? And that men are thus confused and incredulous when women are raped because in their sexual experience women can't be believed? I doubt that this has much to do with men's perceptions of rape. I don't know to what extent women actually "say no and mean yes"; certainly it is a common theme in male folklore. I have spoken to a couple of women who went through periods when they wanted to be sexual but were afraid to be, and often rebuffed initial sexual advances only to give in later. One point is clear: the ambivalence women may feel about having sex is closely tied to the inability of men to fully accept them as sexual beings. Women have been traditionally punished for being openly and freely sexual; men are praised for it. And if many men think of sex as achievement of possession of a valued commodity, or aggressive degradation, then women have every reason to feel and act ambivalent.

Conclusion

A man can grow up in the finest family, get educated at the best schools, call himself literate, humanitarian, and cultured and not once contemplate something fundamental in his experience: women live in social environments far more menacing than men. He can even become a successful psychiatrist and never perceive that the threat of rape constitutes a major mental health issue for all women in American culture.

We cannot count upon the criminal justice system to end rape. If its efficiency were suddenly doubled (an unlikely prospect), not two or three, but four or six of every hundred rapists would find themselves in prison.

For a man to acknowledge and reject all the different ways he has learned to regard women as less than human is an act of courage and an act of love. If violence against women is to end, we will need nothing less than a revolution in consciousness among men. We must create a consciousness that relates to women as people instead of property, that acknowledges and refuses to accept as normal lives of constraint for women, a consciousness that ceases to blame women for rape, and finally a consciousness that is able to acknowledge with clarity its anger at women and put that anger aside.

Notes

1. Such estimates recur in the rape literature. See *Sexual Assault* by Nancy Gager and Cathleen Schurr, Grosset & Dunlap, 1976, or *The Price of Coercive Sexuality* by Clark and Lewis, The Woman's Press, 1977.

2. *Uniform Crime Reports,* 1980.

3. See *Behind Closed Doors* by Murray J. Strauss and Richard Gelles, Doubleday, 1979.

4. See Gager and Schurr (above) or virtually any book on the subject.

5. Again, see Gager and Schurr, or Carol V. Horos, *Rape,* Banbury Books, 1981.

6. From "Willamette Bridge" in *Body Politics* by Nancy Henley, Prentice Hall, 1977, p. 144.

7. This method of analysis is derived from Roland Barthes. See "Myth Today" in *Mythologies,* Hill and Wang, 1979, for a remarkably lucid and subtle exposition.

8. *Journal of Social Issues,* forthcoming.

9. Ibid.

10. I wish to thank George Lakoff for many enlightening discussions on the material in this section.

11. *Metaphors We Live By* by George Lakoff and Mark Johnson, University of Chicago Press, 1980.

12. Ibid., p. 156.

13. *Men Who Rape,* Nicholas Groth, Plenum, 1980, p. 13.

14. Some other sexual assault insults: "Eat me!" "Go fuck yourself!" "Take this job and shove it!" "Up yours!"

15. A tennis star, after winning the tournament at Wimbledon, had difficulties getting along with the English. When they rescinded his invitation to the championship dinner upon his request to arrive late, he said: "The only reason they said it was a big deal was because I won their tournament. That's the only way you can *beat* them . . . that's the only way you could *stick it to them. I stuck it to them real good.*" (Italics mine.) (*San Francisco Chronicle*, July 7, 1981, p. 43.)
    Notice: He invokes "winning is battery"—*he beat them* and "winning is forced aggression"—he *stuck it to them real good.*

16. Women sometimes speak of makeup as "war paint."

17. In using this phrase I don't mean to legitimize oppressive images of prostitution; I only seek to describe a process in men's consciousness.

18. *Dictionary of American Slang,* Harold Wentworth & Stuart B. Flexner, T. Y. Crowell, 1980.

19. *Ms.,* December 1980.

20. Again, I would like to thank George Lakoff.

2

A Variety of Men

"If she'd started crying or something, I would've stopped."

Sam

Eighteen and a freshman in college, he grew up in a small town in Georgia.

I used a little bit of force once where I overpowered a woman. She didn't mind it after it was over. If she'd started crying or something I would've stopped. A lot of it depends upon the situation. If you're with a girl and you're drunk and she's teasing you and leading you on and on and at the very end she says, "No!"—well, if a guy's real drunk, he's gonna lose control and go after her. It's like stopping a hole in a dam with one rock. . . .

A lot of women can look great in anything. Some girls you can tell they're flaunting it and they have power over you. They don't have to wear shirts cut down to their nipples and tight, tight pants. Some of these girls try to flirt with you all the time. I don't know what I'd do if I were in one of their rooms and we were making out and things were hot and heavy and she said, "No." You don't know what you'd do until the situation arises. I had an experience where a woman came back to my room and passed out on the bed beside me and I was sitting there with that evil grin on my face thinking about doing it to her, but I didn't. I guess it differs from person to person. If a guy's got a low tolerance or a heavy sex drive and he's in that situation, he might do it. If you're put in a situation where you can get away with rape, you don't know what you'd do. You just have to be in that situation to find out.

If a guy's not all there to begin with and then he gets fucked over by a couple of girls, he may just have something building up and something will just tick him off about what a girl says and he'll just follow her through the night and rape her.

I can feel for a woman who's been raped. But if you don't know all the circumstances that lead up to it, you don't know for sure what happened.

"It's important to get a man to admit that something he's done, which has involved nominal consent on the part of the woman, is really rape."

Burt

He is a member of Men Against Sexist Violence, a group centered in Berkeley, California, which gives slide shows on sex role stereotyping in media and pornography, and counsels sex offenders and battering men. He is thirty-four and has recently come to perceive a dating experience he had one summer while home from college as, in effect, rape.

I was home from college for the summer and working at a drive-in theater. Judy, who was about fifteen or sixteen, hung out at the theater. She was not part of any social life that I was connected to. She lived in the mountains about fifty miles away and was from a social class and level of education different from what I had. My family had a house deep in the country, and we were part of a middle-class social community that was something like the suburbs.

My father had died by then and my mother and sister were gone for the weekend, so I brought Judy to our house one late summer night. We had a long evening of dinner and talking; later on I wanted to go to bed, and she didn't. We talked about it at length and there was a lot of flattery and cajolery on my part. She was alone in that strange house. I don't think she felt physically threatened by me, at least consciously. My unspoken attitude was: "Well, let's do it or you can't depend on me. If you don't want to go to bed, you're showing that you can't command my esteem or you won't be loved by me." There was that kind of harassment certainly. And this dialogue went on all the way to the bed, and we finally had a kind of loose sexual intercourse. It wasn't violent in a strict physical sense, and in fact didn't really come off: I was nervous and unsure of myself and she was afraid and didn't want penetration really. So it didn't amount to much as a sexual act.

Looking at it now, it seems to me that I had a lot of the attitudes that I've come to distrust in other men. My memory of that evening is that she was verbal, responsive, willing to go a certain way toward having sex, resistent and afraid, but not violently afraid and not afraid I'd leave her or desert her. In examining that memory now, all of my perceptions seem false. She was, in fact, terrified and probably there against her will.

We're taught that rape is forcible and nonconsensual. I think that a lot of rape can also be forcible and *consensual.* In a large number of cases of rape, maybe most, consent is obtained under duress. One way I relate to rape is to think of events like the one with Judy. It's a difference in degree rather than kind, and not even that much a difference in degree.

I had a lot of sympathy and care for Judy, and part of my way of being an estimable person was to distinguish myself from the men she already knew who were abusive and just after sex. But I didn't care enough about her to keep from having sex with her when she didn't really want to. It didn't even *occur* to me. I had no sense of the depths of fear she might experience. My way of relating to her fear was not to stop what I was doing that was making her afraid, but to try to make her less afraid, so I could continue doing what I wanted to do. That's how much I understood. I thought it was perfectly innocent and nonthreatening to go through with this sexual interlude. What I had to do was make her feel okay about it. It wouldn't do to force her. I would have nothing to do with going against her will. Therefore, the thing to do was to get her consent at all costs.

It's what Germaine Greer would call "petty" rape.
   Most of the men I know have done it. It's important to get a man to admit that something he's done which has involved nominal consent on the part of the woman, is really rape. It's a recognition of how widespread rape is, how it's a part of all of us. Operating in me was a belief that I was different from other men, that I wouldn't be involved in such things as rape, certainly not; but I shared at the same time the fundamental male feeling, with regard to Judy, for example, that even if she said no, she'd never mean no and that she could be talked out of it. I felt that way about a number of women I related to. I thought of it as persuasion, clarifying of the facts.
   I grew up in the country and had little to do with my classmates outside school. I was awkward and felt like a terrible social washout in junior and senior high school. I was also a year ahead of my age group and was labeled as the "bright boy"; that contributed to my feeling of isolation. I felt different from other men and didn't particularly seek out their approval (I've since learned that that's what it means to be a man in America—to feel different from other men). But I wanted to be accepted by women: to be thought of as attractive and, in fact, superior to other men. I set

myself up, or got set up by the "society," etc., to be hurt if women didn't approve of me. It wasn't until going to college that I fell in love and began to get the recognition I needed; that changed my life but it didn't change my residual need for recognition from women. During the summer vacation I would hunt for short, safe relationships—for women I could define in advance as socially or educationally inferior, women I could have control over and could leave. Most of it did have to do with needing recognition from women. And behind that unstable need for recognition was a lot of hostility toward women; in principle I could never get enough recognition. That's where I tie in to male feelings of violence toward women, and that's one main form it took in my life.

Just the other day I remembered to my horror an assault that I was part of in the fourth grade. Another boy and I were close friends with a few girls in the grade school and we all played together. At one point the boy, Frank, and I decided we were going to pull down a girl's panties. We planned for it and at a certain prearranged signal during the last recess of the day, we grabbed her and put her down and pulled down her panties. A girl came running up screaming "Stop!"; we each froze, stopped what we were doing, and then ran away, terrified. The whole thing lasted four or five seconds. We felt scared and incredibly ashamed of what we'd done. At a certain point during the assault, Steve and I had become galvanized and stopped thinking about what we were doing. We were curious about her body and aroused at the idea of seeing it. And there was another element: that day we had all been playing together and she was inadvertently showing her underwear; we self-righteously told each other that she was asking for it.

The girl's name was Mary. We'd had a lot of fun playing together for two or three years, but after that it was never the same. I hardly ever saw her in the following eight years we were in school together. There was a complete loss of a good friendship. It was only when I remembered it suddenly the other day after twenty-six years that I even *began* to have a recognition of what she might have gone through, and how it probably altered her life, altered her relation to playmates, to boys, and to men throughout her life.

I felt guilty at the time and guilty for years about it. The guilt was in the service of a morality I no longer believe in. It had nothing to do with the whole issue of violence against women. It was all private, all a sense of wrong, guilt, sin, with no social consciousness. The guilt kept me from trying to understand the process I went through in attempting the assault. It kept me from addressing those feelings and dealing with them.

Last year the activist group I work with, Men Against Sexual Violence, took a trip to Atascadero State Mental Hospital. We went there to interview and spend days on the ward with inmates who were classified as mentally disordered sex offenders.

The first experience I had was blinding: a feeling of *identification*. The men that I met were rapists, child molesters, men who'd molested their own daughters, who had raped sixty-year-old women; and they were not different from the men I knew. They could've been my brother, could've been my father, could've been my friends, could've been *me*.

My group had a lot of theories about male conditioning in this society that we'd gotten from following the women's movement and doing our own work. An inmate at Atascadero has a lot of explanations of why he did what he did and those explanations sounded plausible to us. But at the same time he has something we didn't count as part of our ideology.

Whether because he's behind bars and forced to confront what he's done or whether he's adopting a rhetoric to get out soon, an inmate at Atascadero is compelled to take responsibility for what he did. I couldn't understand this at the time, but I'm beginning to get a sense of it. The men would come to us and say, "I'm responsible, I did it, and I have to make my life better. I have to make changes." It sounded to me like a rebirth of machoism: "I have to go it alone, etc." Now I see that it's important to recognize the fact of violence against women in your life, to find it and recognize it as a global phenomenon that runs throughout your life. And it's important for politicizing and educating yourself and other people to come up with reasons why you had the anger. But it's *more* important to realize that you *had* it: that you did what you did and were a part of this violence against women in your own life. It doesn't matter whether you did what *I* did, or did downright stranger-to-stranger rape, or did assault or verbal harassment. The point is to recognize it as *your* act and, in the process of recognizing it as your act, to recognize that *you're* free to change it.

That's what guilt might positively mean—instead of letting it immobilize you, let it give you a sense of power and freedom. Those guys at Atascadero had it figured out much better than we did. They were forced to take responsibility, not just in the sense of guilt or repentance, but to take charge of their lives, to understand when the violence is coming, and to do something about it, and to know that they—that *we*—must never do it again, *never* do it again.

"Just the fact that they can come up to me and just melt me and make me feel like a dummy makes me want revenge."

Jay

He is twenty-three, grew up in Pittsburgh, and works as a file clerk in the financial district of San Francisco.

Where I work it's probably no different from any other major city in the U.S. The women dress up in high heels, and they wear a lot of makeup, and they just look really *hot* and really sexy, and how can somebody who has a healthy sex drive not feel lust for them when you see them? I feel lust for them, but I don't think I could find it in me to overpower someone and rape them. But I definitely get the feeling that I'd like to rape a girl. I don't know if the actual act of rape would be satisfying, but the *feeling* is satisfying.

These women look so good, and they kiss ass of the men in the three-piece suits who are *big* in the corporation, and most of them relate to me like "Who are *you*? Who are *you* to even *look* at?" They're snobby and they condescend to me, and I resent it. It would take me a lot longer to get to first base than it would somebody with a three-piece suit who had money. And to me a lot of the men they go out with are superficial assholes who have no real feelings or substance, and are just trying to get ahead and make a lot of money. Another thing that makes me resent these women is thinking, "How could she want to hang out with somebody like that? What does that make her?"

I'm a file clerk, which makes me feel like a nebbish, a nurd, like I'm not making it, I'm a failure. But I don't really believe I'm a failure because I know it's just a phase, and I'm just doing it for the money, just to make it through this phase. I catch myself feeling like a failure, but I realize that's ridiculous.

What exactly do you go through when you see these sexy, unavailable women?

Let's say I see a woman and she looks really pretty and really clean and sexy, and she's giving off very feminine, sexy vibes. I think, "Wow, I would love to make love to her," but I know she's not really interested. It's a tease. A lot of times a woman knows that she's looking really good and she'll use that and flaunt it, and it makes me feel like she's laughing at me and I feel *degraded*.

I also feel dehumanized, because when I'm being teased I just turn off, I cease to be human. Because if I go with my human emotions I'm going to want to put my arms around her and kiss her, and to do that would be unacceptable. I don't like the feeling that I'm supposed to stand there and take it, and not be able to hug her or kiss her; so I just turn off my emotions. It's a feeling of humiliation, because the woman has forced me to turn off my feelings and react in a way that I really don't want to.

If I were actually desperate enough to rape somebody, it would be from wanting the person, but also it would be a very spiteful thing, just being able to say, "I have power over you and I can do anything I want with you," because really I feel that *they* have power over *me* just by their presence. Just the fact that they can come up to me and just melt me and make me feel like a dummy makes me want revenge. They have power over me so I want power over them. . . .

Society says that you have to have a lot of sex with a lot of different women to be a real man. Well, what happens if you don't? Then what are you? Are you half a man? Are you still a boy? It's ridiculous. You see a whiskey ad with a guy and two women on his arm. The implication is that real men don't have any trouble getting women.

How does it make you feel toward women to see all these sexy women in media and advertising using their looks to try to get you to buy something?

It makes me hate them. As a man you're taught that men are more powerful than women, and that men always have the upper hand, and that it's a man's society; but then you see all these women and it makes you think, "Jesus Christ, if we have all the power how come all the beautiful women are telling us what to buy?" And to be honest, it just makes me hate beautiful women because they're using their power over me. I realize they're being used themselves, and they're doing it for the money. In *Playboy* you see all these beautiful women who look so sexy and they'll be giving you all these looks like they want to have sex so bad; but then in reality you know that except for a few nymphomaniacs, they're doing it for the money; so I hate them for being used and for using their bodies in that way.

In this society, if you ever sit down and realize how manipulated you really are it makes you pissed off—it makes you want to take control. And you've been manipulated by women, and they're a very easy target because they're out walking along the streets, so you can just grab one and say, "Listen, you're going to do what I want you to do," and it's an act of revenge against the way you've been manipulated.

I know a girl who was walking down the street by her house, when this guy jumped her and beat her up and raped her, and she was black and blue and had to go to the hospital. That's beyond me. I can't understand how somebody could do that. If I were going to rape a girl, I wouldn't hurt her. I might *restrain* her, but I wouldn't *hurt* her. . . .

The whole dating game between men and women also makes me feel degraded. I hate being put in the position of having to initiate a relationship. I've been taught that if you're not aggressive with a woman, then you've blown it. She's not going to jump on *you*, so *you've* got to jump on *her*. I've heard all kinds of stories where the woman says, "No! No! No!" and they end up making great love. I get confused as hell if a woman pushes me away. Does it mean she's trying to be a nice girl and wants to put up a good appearance, or does it mean she doesn't want anything to do with you? You don't know. Probably a lot of men think that women don't feel like real women unless a man tries to force himself on her, unless she brings out the "real man," so to speak, and probably too much of it goes on. It goes on in my head that you're complimenting a woman by actually staring at her or by trying to get into her pants. Lately, I'm realizing that when I stare at women lustfully, they often feel more threatened than flattered.

"I feel that too much is expected of me because I'm a man."

Rick

He grew up in a small town in South Carolina and studied English in college, where he reviewed movies for the campus newspaper. He has worked as a bartender, an operating room technician, and currently works as a carpenter. He is thirty-two.

I met a woman where I worked who I asked out for a drink and we had several drinks, and I asked her if she wanted to come home with me and she said she would come over and listen to music if I promised not to rape her, and I said sure. We went home and drank some more, and listened to music, and I asked her if she wanted to stay and she said she would, but I had to promise not to rape her, and I said fine.

So I took off my pants and shirt and kept on my underclothes and went to bed, and she went into the bathroom and came out in her bra and panties and threw them off and crawled into bed and grabbed me. We played around for a while, but finally I said *enough,* because she was drunker than I was and she seemed disappointed. I said the "right thing," that she would "understand" tomorrow and that she would thank me, and we went to sleep and the next day she was very thankful.

Later on she told me how, when I had met her, she was bouncing around from this man who had raped her, and she had also been raped by one of her professors. That night she was with me, if we had gone ahead and had sex it would have been much closer to her raping me than me raping her, but she's the woman so she can cry rape. If we had had sex that night, I don't think she would've cried rape the next day, but later on she probably would have looked back on it as a rape. I rather suspect that with either of the two people she had said raped her that she didn't regard it as a rape the next day, but looking back on it long afterward she called it rape.

That personal experience makes me wonder about what many women call rape. The thing that throws me is the offhand fashion with which I've heard women talk about rape. I just don't think I could go through anything that traumatic and be that offhand about it. It just seemed a few years ago that a lot of women had to have a rape story and the way women would talk about it confused me. . . .

I feel that too much is expected of me because I'm a man. It's like being pulled in two directions. You're torn between the precepts you as a man were raised with, that you're supposed to be dominant and a provider and be very deferential and respectful to women. If you're deferential to women it may be accepted graciously or you may get put down for it. You get it both ways and you don't know how to direct yourself. The women's movement has opened men's eyes to the dangers of sex roles and stereotypes, but it's confused and frustrated a lot of men, and I think that's contributed to the rise of rape.

A lot of women are affected by the women's movement and want to sway both ways. They want the independence and at the same time want a shelter and a support, and sway back and forth almost day by day. And, for me, trying to figure out which day is which, which day the woman wants me to be strong and lean on me, and which day she wants to be independent and resents my being strong, is frustrating. As the "oppressor," I'm the one who has to behave in the right fashion. The woman has been oppressed and that excuses many of her actions. And, on top of that, I don't feel like I'm an oppressor.

Dealing with what I feel are contradictory messages from women has put me in such a state that often I don't take seriously the cries of women that are probably valid. It's desensitized me to the legitimate complaints that women have, and that may to some degree include their complaints about rape. Sometimes because of the conflicting messages I get personally, I feel ambivalent and frustrated as hell toward women, and I think that someone who was not as analytical, or less in control emotionally than I am, could easily be violent or rape. When women speak in angry terms of males as oppressors and rapists I resent being lumped together with them. It's the same mentality that talks about all blacks being shiftless and lazy.

". . . too many freebies."

Hank

He's around forty and lives in Oakland, California.

We don't have any rape around here, there's too many freebies. We don't have that problem around here unless you're sick and I don't mess with sick people. If you're sick you might rape somebody, but there's too many women around here who are gonna give it away free. So why should a man rape unless he's sick? If he's some kind of fanatic he's going to go rape somebody. . . .

"It's sort of rotten. It's like the only way you can get sex is by spoiling it for yourself."

Mike

He is a thirty-year-old writer, editor, and translator who lives in Berkeley, California.

Sometimes I feel like the available alternatives are to be strong, aggressive, and inconsiderate and do well with women, or to be weak, considerate, and a eunuch. It's almost as if to be powerful, you have to be insensitive. You're forced to be aggressive even though you don't want to be.

A few weeks ago I met this woman Nancy; there was an immediate bond between us. We got to know each other and she said she didn't want to get sexually involved. That was okay. I wasn't upset by it, but it puzzled me because I sensed ambivalence in what she said. After she said it she looked me very deeply in the eyes; I had a strong feeling that she was confused and seeking some kind of response from me. I felt puzzled and asked her if she was sure. She looked really unhappy; not angry, but just troubled. So I said, "I'm sorry, I guess this is difficult for you." She said, "Yes," so I let it slide.

Later I saw her and we stayed up until four-thirty in the morning. She told me her life story and really confided in me; I felt flattered. I can't tell if it's projection on my part, but I felt she wanted me to hug her and be really affectionate. I was being warm and friendly without being physical, not so much out of consideration for her but out of fear of rejection. It was getting to the point where I felt like kissing her and then she got very quiet and told me she had gotten involved with John, a friend of mine. I felt angry and said, "Why do you wait until the end of the evening when I'm all worked up? Why didn't you tell me earlier?" I'm all worked up and then I'm presented with an inhibiting factor. As soon as I said that, she started kissing me. That was all right. I didn't understand it; I didn't know what was going on or how to deal with it. It's hard to say, "Stop! I don't know what's going on" when somebody's kissing you.

So I went home and decided not to worry about it. After that she wanted to see me more and more. I thought, Well, maybe this is just something she has to do to feel relaxed. Maybe she has to reject me so she'll feel comfortable enough to start seeing me. It gives her control. Since she told me she doesn't want to be involved sexually, then I'm not allowed to do anything, so she's always in control. That's a standard thing for women to do. But it's hard for me to believe she could be that calculating because she's so innocent and young.

Last night she comes for dinner, and I have made a significant repression. I've decided it's best to keep it on a friendship level because I'm not quite sure if she's really interested in sleeping with me. So we had dinner and it was all very sweet and she had a paper to write and I helped her with it. She was going to work on her paper and I had some writing to do, so we were going to sit at the table and work.

But she's not working on her paper. She's just chatting incessantly with me and I don't know what's going on. It gets to be four in the morning and I've managed to pump out five or ten pages.

Pump out?

Maybe "pump out" means something because all this time I'm sublimating. Anyway, I say, "Look, you look like you're falling asleep. Maybe you ought to take a nap." She said, "Maybe for twenty minutes. Should I go to sleep in the chair?" I said, "Am I sleeping in the bed? No. Why don't you use the bed." And then she looked *depressed.* So I said, "If you want, I'll sit there and tell you a story and you can doze off and I'll wake you in twenty minutes." She liked that. Something she definitely likes.

So we go into the bedroom and she's giving me cute little looks and I tell her a weird little story and she laughed pretty hard and I told her to go to sleep. She was like a kid. So I sat there and felt very tender in the dark and she said, "If you're bored, you can go." I said, "I just feel kind of peaceful. But my heart's pounding. Things haven't changed since I was seventeen." And there's a little chatter going on and we're hugging a little bit and there's no doubt in my mind that we're looking forward to this. When I say "we" I mean my split personality: the one part that doesn't want to get involved in a situation that's ambiguous, and the other part that likes her and doesn't care, that wants to go for it. It's rare that I feel this physically attracted to someone and I definitely feel it with this woman, so I'm going to do it if I can and if she wants me.

So I lay down in bed with her. She took my hand and said, "I don't want to lead you on." It was said in a way that confused me. I didn't take it as a sexual rejection. Then she was intensely affectionate with me. She started hugging me and kissing me intensely. I didn't quite know what was happening. I felt intensely passionate and I think she did, too. Since she wasn't stopping I thought, "Maybe she's afraid to hurt my feelings. Maybe she likes me a lot and doesn't know how to handle the situation. She may genuinely want to make love with me. At the same time I really don't know that. It's possible that if I really start kissing her she'll submit, but I won't like it because I won't be able to be sure if she's just doing it so as not to hurt my feelings, and then it'll be an act of submission on her part and I won't want to do that."

So I withdrew and she drifted off to sleep; I went into the other room and felt sad. And a few minutes later she woke up and came back in. I felt really stirred up sexually and wanted to be alone to let it subside. I was sort of angry that it didn't happen. I didn't want her to see me because I felt vulnerable and ashamed.

She seemed upset. I said, "Look, it's all right. We had this misunderstanding. We didn't get angry. It didn't come to a point where I was kissing you and you said stop. I wouldn't want you to do something you wouldn't want to do." I think if she'd known how turned on I was, she would've been frightened.

If you'd been aggressive and pushy and bullying, you might have had sex with her?

Yes, but I felt that I didn't want to force anything on her. I felt that if she wants me that's fine, but if she doesn't really know if she wants me, then what do I do? I didn't want to kill my own spontaneity. If I felt I was forcing her in any way, I wouldn't be able to have sex with her. If forcing her was the only way to have sex with her I wouldn't be able to do it.

Part of me felt like she was a coward. Instead of saying she was teasing me or leading me on, my way of interpreting it is to say that she was a coward. I thought, This could've been amazing. You don't have the courage to do what you really want to because it's too threatening. You're a coward.

Have you been in situations where the woman submitted to your aggression rather than genuinely consented?

Yes, definitely, with June, my old girlfriend. After I'd broken up with another woman I made a decision to get involved with her. I'd been attracted to her and just went out and found her and asked her out. The first night we dated she was willing to stay at my house. We were riding with my friend in a car and I said, "Oh, well, we'll take you home." My friend was amazed and said to me, "Are you kidding? You're willing to take her home? You're not going to take her home and fuck her? I can't believe it. That's what she wants. That's what she's waiting for."

I said, "I like her. I don't feel that way about her. I just want to get to know her. I don't want her to think that all I want to do is take her out and fuck her." So I waited until the next night. Except I really didn't have that idea until my friend planted it in my head. In saying that, I'm trying to get out of it, I guess. But when he said that, it was an indictment of my manhood and I felt threatened by it. It was like: What's the matter with you? What kind of a man are you?

As if a "real man" wouldn't turn down a sexual opportunity. You're supposed to be ready at all times.

Especially if that's what the woman wants. So the next night she came over and we had dinner together and started making out. She was into it; she wasn't passive, but afterward I could tell that she was unhappy about it because she hadn't wanted it so soon. She was spooked. She wanted to do it but she would've been happier if there'd been a courtship.

I had psyched myself up and said I'm not going to have my conscience enter into this, because in the past it always did. It was a real attempt to do things differently from the way I normally did them.

Your conscience is that part of you that respects what the woman is feeling?

Or *might* be feeling. I was cynical. I was going to take this woman and give her what she wanted. I was feeling totally cynical and thought, I've always courted women and romantic courtship is *bullshit.* The thing that gets between people is this romanticized notion of sex. We'll just have sex and get it out of the way and we'll be human beings.

I felt extremely guilty the next day because I'd never done anything like that before. I'd never taken charge of a situation. I'd been getting a lot of pressure from male friends to take charge with women—"You have to fuck them and not worry about it. It's important to fuck them because that's what they want. You can't be wishy-washy or respectful or considerate. They won't like that. They'll think you're not potent then. That's mainly what they want no matter what they say."

Do you think there's any truth in that?

I think there's *some* truth in that. I wish there weren't. It's sort of rotten. It's like the only way you can get sex is by spoiling it for yourself.

"There has to be some point in every rape where the woman relaxes and enjoys it."

Joe

He is nineteen and a freshman in college. He lives in a small town in Alabama.

I think I could be provoked enough to rape a girl. But it would be her fault for provoking me. She'd have to push me pretty hard. If I was on a date and she grabbed my dick, I could lose control. If she wants to touch it, she should want it. I'm not saying it's okay to do it, but if a woman grabs you, you *feel* like doing it. If I were provoked enough to rape a girl, she would have to do something just as bad as what I did to make me do it. I can see how a guy could do it, but I guess girls don't see that. That's why girls think it's so bad and have such a different opinion. If I were to rape, it would be out of lust but it would also be because I was angry.

When you see a girl walking around wearing real skimpy clothes, she's offending you and I guess rape would be a way of getting even. If I'm on a date and a girl's dressing sexy and acting sexy, why doesn't she want to have sex? The whole time you figure she's going to say yes because she's teasing you, and all of a sudden she switches because she's going to save it for marriage or something. That's not right. She shouldn't have lead you on in the first place.

You see girls walking around in their little shorts and halter tops, flaunting it, and when guys whistle at them, a lot of times they respond back. The women who say they feel humiliated when a guy whistles at them: deep down they really like it, it's boosting their egos. . . .

There has to be some point in every rape where the woman relaxes and enjoys it. I'm not saying that ladies *want* to be raped *because* they enjoy it, but there has to be some point where they enjoy it, because it's enjoyable. Sex is enjoyable. There has to be some pleasure in it. And if they're walking around asking for it, in my opinion they deserve it. Maybe not deserve it, but it's inevitable. If you walk the streets at night or any time wearing skimpy shit, sooner or later you're going to get nailed. It's like you walk through some slum with a pocketful of money—sooner or later you're going to get robbed. You should've known better than to do that in the first place. I don't feel a bit of sympathy for people who do stupid things like that.

If a woman came up to me and said she was just raped, I

would not believe her. I'd be real suspicious. I'd think if a girl's been raped, she wouldn't say it to me in the first place; she'd be at the police department already. If a woman walked up to me with a low-cut blouse and said she'd been raped, the first thing I'd think would be, "sure," and the second thing I'd think would be, "you asked for it by walking around in skimpy clothes." I would have more sympathy for a woman who was fully dressed who got raped. If my mom or sister were raped, I'd probably lose my head, but I know they're not going to go around flaunting it. They're not going to *get* raped. . . .

When you have a steady girlfriend or if you're married, girls will flirt with you just to give you that enraged temptation. They know you're not going to do anything to them, so they're going to push real hard to make you real mad. They're trying to show that they can rule a guy, that they can get it when they want and you can't. That's the thing that bugs me, that they can get it when they want and you can't. There's a frustration because everybody but James Bond doesn't get enough, and he doesn't really get it. But any girl, any time—I don't care if she's five foot four and 350 pounds—can go out and get fucked; but a guy sure can't, at least I can't when I want to. And that just makes you mad.

It's like women being equal to men. I don't think it will ever happen. They may be able to do it all right now. A lot of girls can do a job better than I can but they just won't. Because when it comes down to it, if a girl wants to, she can live off a guy. But no guy is born with the idea that some day he can grow up and live off a girl.

How do you feel about getting married?

She better be damn good. I want to have a wife I can come home to. They got it real easy. A girl gets it real easy. I feel better when I'm supporting a girl because I want a girl who's going to be helpless. I don't want some domineering bitch who's going to take care of herself and be an executive and make more money than me. That'll make me mad; I'll get divorced real quick if she makes more money than I do.

How do you feel about the issue of rape in marriage?

If a guy has to rape his wife, she ought to consider something that she's doing wrong. It's not just going to be one night that he wants it so bad he has to rape her. She's gotta be puttin' it off for a good while before a husband will rape his wife.

The only time it should ever be considered rape is if a guy jumps out of nowhere and rapes a woman. In dating rape or marital rape, the lady is just as much at fault for getting the guy going in the first place.

I guess in any rape some of it's the woman's fault. Some of it has to be. She shouldn't have allowed herself to be in the position to get raped. Nobody throws you down on the sidewalk and rapes you. I'm not saying all rapes are caused by women. I'm saying they play a part in it and have a responsibility. Whenever I picture rape, I picture Central Park in New York and a lady walking along and somebody jumping from a bush and getting her. I don't picture a plumber doing it in a house. Even if it was a guy in a plumber's suit, it's the lady's fault for letting him in.

Girls are saying how bad it is and how hard it is to prove, and how traumatic; I guess it is pretty bad for a girl if she gets raped. But if they made the laws more in favor of the victim, they'd abuse it worse than the men abuse it right now by raping. A girl can get you to do it with her and then the next day she changes her mind and cries rape.

Rape cases are touchy. Anybody in a rape case is ruined for life unless they live off somebody else. Like if I was a successful businessman and some girl says I raped her, you're going to be ruined even if you're innocent. That's the thing that scares me about making liberal rape laws where it's easier to get a conviction.

To girls it's just that experience. When a guy thinks about it, he's worried about what's going to happen later on. I'm not saying a girl can forget about it, but she can live and be successful because all the sympathy goes to the girl. If some girl cries rape on you, people think you're crazy and a lot of times I guess you're not. Women get sympathy if it happens to them—"Ah, the poor lady." It's not held against them. At least I don't hold it against them.

"They have to feel like, 'I can force myself upon a woman, so I'm a man.' "

Ernie

He's in his late twenties and works in construction in northern California.

I had a sister that was forced upon and she developed this real low outlook on herself. She didn't turn against men in general, but like now she needs a man around constantly to feel safe. I was young at the time it happened and there was a noticeable difference. She had a lot of hatred in her from it and that came because of the fear. She didn't have no way of expressing the fear she felt and she just turned it into hatred. It's been about thirteen years since it happened and she's coming out of it now but she still has that need for a protector. Her hatred and fears are kind of subsided to a degree, I guess from coming to some sort of an understanding toward herself. She wants to have the affection of men but she's kind of apprehensive about it. . . .

Why do men make jokes about women who've been raped?
   The guys who say things like, "Well, she deserved it," or "She was asking for it," or who don't seem to think about the way it went down, are just expressing their own insecurity about their manhood. They have to feel like, "I can force myself upon a

woman, so I'm a man," or "Someone else can force himself upon a woman and I can see it and say well that's cool," or justify it in some kind of way. They think that makes them a man, when all in all, it doesn't. They're trying to convince themselves of their manhood or trying to convince someone else that they are a man, when all in all, they have some type of insecurity in them.

It's like the man who drinks a keg of beer at a party to prove that "I'm the toughest, I drank a keg of beer," when in actuality he's the drunkest and the biggest fool. It's a way of proving yourself.

"Vietnamese women were made into objects of fear and dread, and it was easy to feel angry at them."

Daniel

Now a psychologist, he spent a year with the Marines in Vietnam in 1967. He is thirty-two.

A Viet Cong woman had been wounded and was taken prisoner by a Navy corpsman and the following morning we heard the story that this Navy corpsman and one or two other soldiers had tried to rape her, and when she resisted they put their fingers in the wound in her back, and tried to probe into her lungs to get her to submit.

My friends and I reacted with disgust and anger. There was nothing we could do about it because he'd already done it. No one that I knew thought it was a decent thing to do, though the attitude of this Navy corpsman and the people who helped him was obviously different. I wish I could remember his name. It was

First Battalion, Third Marines in Vietnam around May 1967. This Navy corpsman was formerly a Marine, so that's enough information if he should be identified.

There was a lot of group pressure against rape. Some soldiers, who were really psychopathic personalities, could commit rape, especially in less controlled situations. I heard a lot of rumors about Vietnam women: they had razor blades in their vaginas and if you had sex with them you'd get castrated; they had black syphilis, which was supposedly incurable; they were Viet Cong agents. Vietnamese women were made into objects of fear and dread, and it was easy to feel angry at them. The stories about razor blades seemed plausible to me at the time. I didn't consider the physical logistics of keeping a razor in the vagina. Now I see it as a reflection of a pervasive castration anxiety among soldiers.

The American male presence in Vietnam resulted in the rape of the values and well-being of the Vietnamese people, their culture, every aspect of their living. We raped their land, abused them, denigrated them, projected the negative aspects of ourselves onto them. *That* is rape, the rape of the human soul. And I'm sure a fair amount of literal rape happened, too.

"I definitely felt played with, used, manipulated, like women were testing their power over me."

Stan

He is single, in his mid-thirties, and has held a variety of jobs.

Growing up, I definitely felt teased by women. I think for the most part women knew when I was attracted to them so women would sit a certain way or give a three-quarter beaver shot or give you a little bit of tit and maybe not give much more, or lift their skirts a certain way or rub their breasts into me. I definitely felt played with, used, manipulated, like women were testing their power over me. I hated it with a passion! With a *fucking* passion! I wanted to slam someone's head up against a wall.

Up until the last couple of years, women had a sense of trust that I wouldn't violate them; not that they've given up that trust, but now I let myself be aggressive if I'm feeling aggressive and there's a connection between me and the woman, whereas before I've always felt guilty about being aggressive.

The type of teasing that's done to me now isn't coming from an unsympathetic noncaring place. There's a certain manipulation but not as much as there used to be. It bothers me when I see women manipulating and teasing; when women sit a certain way, or try to manipulate somebody into buying them a drink, or taking it for granted that they should be taken care of. I hate that. I almost have the feeling that men are more desperate than women. Women can lay back and have more of a choice about who will come after them. I've had a lot of envy and jealousy that women can just do that and have so many men because it's so powerful. I've felt belittled by that power, belittled because they can't see who I am or feel who I am because they're able to use their body as a way of attracting men through being flirtatious or coming on or whatever.

I've always felt powerless to come on to a woman who was being that sexual. A good example is the woman I'm with now. At one time the only way she knew how to relate to a man was by being sexual and being a real flirt. I had the hardest time being me when I first met her. I was attracted to her but at the same time intimidated. She had all this power. She knew how to use her body in a certain way and unless I could meet her standards sexually and in being psychologically together, I wasn't going to be able to fit the bill. It wasn't until I brought it up to her that I thought she used sex as the only way to relate to men that we got to know each other better.

But even now she can still use her body to distract me. Unless I'm feeling very strong about something I want to talk about, she can lure me into bed. When that happens, I generally feel an emptiness afterward. I really need a lot of affection. Affection means more to me than being able to sleep with somebody. If I ask for affection from a woman I'm seeing and they're unable or unwilling to give it, that hurts me and makes me more angry than anything else. It's almost as if by not showing affection a woman can be manipulative and teasing. It almost appears that way, though it's not black and white.

Where else does your anger at women come from?

My general anger at women comes from the way I was brought up, the way women were put on a pedestal, were considered pure, deemed worthy of total respect whereas I wasn't given any respect; from seeing how they had control in situations over their husbands. Never really being active sexually when I was younger made me feel more and more intimidated. So when I'm around a woman who has a certain sense of power but who has no gentleness and no compassion, that makes me angry. She's manipulating, totally manipulating, and I have a real hard time with that. I feel like I want to belt her, throw her against a wall or through a window. She's not being sensitive at all to me; she's not being sensitive to my feelings; she's not picking up my caring; she doesn't understand and perceive how I want to share something about my life, how I want to care about her. When that happens it just destroys me and I feel ripped inside and I feel like ripping her apart both sexually and physically. The image I've always had is of a woman holding the faucet over the bathtub and seeing her cheeks spread from the back and ramming it right in there. It's wanting to get out my aggressions, let out a lot of sexual frustration and rage. One of my favorite images is making love in the sand dunes and just seeing the indentation of somebody I've just fucked about two and a half feet down. It's like total power.

Too often I've had experiences where a woman has been turned on and she'll rationalize and decide she doesn't want to have sex. That second guessing when things seem to be flowing really rips me apart. I guess my fantasy of ripping her apart is a kind of revenge.

A lot of times my anger is frustration with myself that gets vented toward women. It comes from feeling rather powerless most of my life, having trouble getting a good job making money, being unable to feel what I wanted to feel, feeling humiliated and embarrassed, feeling like an outsider looking in.

Have you known women who've been raped?

I've never been close to a women who's been raped, so I've never shared much about rape with a woman. When I think about rape I think how women aren't as strong as men, they're going to be physically intimidated; in the sexual revolution with so much emphasis on being free and letting out your inhibitions. Women who've been dishonest about their feelings are not going to know how to deal with that issue.

A lot of times, I think there's a lot of mental rape that gets pent up in women's heads. What comes to mind is walking the streets of Amsterdam with my sister and a girlfriend of hers and she was saying how "men are this, men are that, men are animals." Well, not animals; she was more liberated than a lot of women I've met. If she was being looked at by a man, she would almost turn around with her fist clenched as if to say, "Who the fuck are you looking at?" When you send out vibes like that it doesn't promote world harmony. It just makes things worse.

Was she being harassed?

To me it wasn't anything to get that upset about. I guess it depends upon what you're used to. I was traveling with a Swiss woman in Italy and she said, "If I went to Italy and didn't expect to get pinched a few times I'd be nuts; I wouldn't have a good time, it's going to happen." It has a lot to do with your acceptance of the culture. . . .

If there's a sensitivity and openness to talk about what's going on, a lot of hostility and fantasies and even rape would be alleviated. I know that a lot of women don't want to hear about those fantasies and feelings. It's really tricky. What do you share? Where do you draw the line? I could see women not wanting to deal with it if they feel scared. Women are so fucking intimidated! A recent girlfriend of mine said that when she looked at me at times she almost didn't want to be in the same room because she felt that I could explode and belt her or kill her at any time.

I was wrestling recently with a girlfriend of mine and getting out a lot of frustration and anger and trying to get some stuff out of her—"Just what are you feeling, fucker?" I was on top of her and I wouldn't get off for nearly an hour and she was really unwilling to test her own power. I know in other situations she is as strong as a fucker, but when it really came down to fighting and standing on her own two feet, she wouldn't do it. There's an awful lot of physical intimidation and I don't know how conscious most women are about it or if they're willing to admit how it scars them emotionally.

"I can be sitting there reading about some gang rape and right-eously thinking how horrifying it is, while discovering to my own amazement that there is a rip-roaring bulge in my pants."

Mark

He is in his mid-forties and has worked (among other things) as a social worker, a photo editor for a national men's magazine, and a cab driver.

Rape turns me on vicariously. It has a definite appeal. I am excited by reading about it, by seeing it in movies. Not the actualization of it, but the fantasy of it turns me on. I don't have a classic macho attitude. I almost identify with the victim in a masochistic way. My fantasies are not of violent rape, but more of forcing someone to submit and then get into the enjoyment of sex. To me it very much boils down to a matter of will. A woman is brought up to believe that willfully a woman is not supposed to enjoy sex, so the whole mythos has us forcing women against their will to submit to something that they will ultimately enjoy, and then the pleasure will take over, which is our definition of sin. . . .

Perhaps I should state clearly here that I think that anyone who actually rapes a woman, or a man, or in any way forces someone to have sex should have their balls cut off; I mean literally castrated!

A lot of my fantasies are an outgrowth of either pornographic movies or literature. I don't have that rich an S/M fantasy life per se anymore. I used to as a kid. I don't know how much that has to do with growing up in a war mentality in World War II, hearing what the Nazis were doing to the Jewish people, and what the Japanese soldiers were doing to prisoners of war, in the way of sexual torture.

Much of my early rape fantasies were to imagine raping the female Nazi camp guards, slowly and with great relish. I was doing it to righteously punish these vicious blond Brunhildas for what they had done to others. I can't just aggressively rape someone. I must rescue victims by aggressively raping their attackers.

I no longer have these fantasies, and maybe that's why it turns me on to read about it or see it in movies. I can be sitting there reading about some gang rape and righteously thinking how horrifying it is, while discovering to my own amazement that there is a rip-roaring bulge in my pants.

One of my favorite fantasies from literature is the gang rape. There is something unbelievably appealing to me, that really turns me on, about two or three men holding down a woman while the fourth sexually assaults her, and then taking turns. Sometimes I identify with the victim, and sometimes I am each one of the four guys. . . .

In my own fantasies, I'm more of a seducer than a rapist, although in real life, I never try to convince a woman to sleep with me who's not already sure whether she wants to. I remember once, in the middle of some steamy necking with someone's wife, she suddenly jumped up and said "I'm feeling guilty!", perhaps expecting me to say something reassuring. However, I said, "Goodbye, call me when you've got it worked out." And I took her home. I just can't deal with that kind of ambivalence.

Rape movies where the rape is an erotic fantasy kind of rape are an incredible turn-on to me. Such films as the opening sex scene in "Last Tango in Paris," or the rapes in "Billy Joe" and especially "Straw Dogs." I also like those films that show a woman forcibly protesting while becoming more and more turned on viscerally as the rape proceeds, despite her protestations.

I'm fascinated, while at the same time repelled, by the idea of snuff films, which supposedly come out of South America, where women are allegedly raped, tortured, mutilated, and killed. Although I've never seen one, I think: What could be more bizarre, let me see it some more so that I can be turned off by it. I should also add here that during my teens, after I had moved along from Nazis, I discovered the writings of de Sade. I was disgusted, amused, provoked, and ultimately very, very turned on.

Why do you think you have these fantasies? Where do they come from in you?

I can't go any further than to say: because they give me an erection. Why do they give me an erection? I don't know how to answer that. Why do I like the taste of steak? I'm not sure it *can* be answered, other than to say that it's psychobiological, or something like that.

In my fantasies there are only certain women I want to rape; bad women, evil women, sometimes aloof women. I want to give them a taste of their own medicine. I want to punish them. Maybe I want to rape a woman who would not willingly sleep with me, who would be condescending to me, who would not notice me sexually. There's an element of class resentment in that perhaps. There might also be an element of "She won't respect me unless I force her."

In my fantasy of rape, it's sort of like a medieval torture technique, where they tease death slowly from a person; I refine it to where I am teasing a woman's sexuality out of her against her will. In my wilder fantasies, I bypass conventional social reality and get down to the gut animal level of creating a "bitch in heat."

Has something gone wrong in a culture when sensitive men of good conscience can be turned on by rape? Should our moral revulsion at rape inhibit our sexuality?

No, it's just the opposite. Our society has striven to repress those very feelings. It wasn't until Freud and Havelock Ellis that there was an acknowledgment that these sadistic, often violent fantasies really do exist in normal people, including children. Freud said that sadomasochistic fantasies are so prevalent in children that they can't be considered abnormal; that they're a way of working out feelings of revenge, and all kinds of stuff. . . .

Society has made it so I have to rationalize and justify these feelings. . . . Since I cannot justify the turn-on of rape per se, my mental victims would become evil, terrible Nazis, etc., that are simply getting their just deserts. . . .

I once knew a woman who wanted me to rape her to prove a point. She was a very bright woman, a radical feminist, who was taking the intellectual position that a man could wear down a woman's resistance in a strictly physical sense very quickly; that he could simply outlast her, and that a woman submitting to a man without struggling is not doing it willingly, but because she's simply run out of energy. This woman put me to the test by asking me to rape her, literally to force her to the bed and force her legs apart and to keep struggling with her until I wore down her resistance, which she was convinced would cave in before I wore out. She initially put up a fierce struggle, which I simply matched, without trying to overpower her, and sure enough, her energy was totally drained in a very short time (two or three minutes), while I hadn't even gone to my reserve energy yet. Maybe because it was a controlled situation and because I was someone she trusted we both ended up getting very turned on and had some very good high-energy sex.

A lot of men persist in believing that no women can be raped even though a woman can be overpowered and even though in most rape cases physical threat is involved.

That's what many men would like to think because it's a great justification for scapegoating the woman. Men want to scapegoat women, because they're afraid of women, afraid of being devoured, oppressed, afraid of being controlled, afraid of being humiliated and shamed, which incidentally are some of the weapons I have seen women use in the eternal battle of the sexes. In this never-ending struggle for supremacy, or even just for equalizing, the only weapons available to many men are physical force and money. . . .

The fear of aggressive women may be important in understanding rape. A fifties shibboleth said if you want to avoid being raped, just aggressively start kissing and stroking the guy and he'll be turned off. There's no reason to suppose that would actually happen. The theory behind it is that he's looking for something else, namely a woman he can overwhelm. . . .

Are there women who want to be raped?

What's confusing our thinking is that there is a certain type of woman who does want to be raped, at least in fantasy. I would suggest that no woman wants to be raped in a way that she has no control over.

But if she is in control, is that really rape, really against her will?

The woman has a preset determination of what rape is, and if the right person comes along and does just the right thing, she might like it. She doesn't know what's going to happen and that's what makes it exciting, as long as it doesn't get out of her control.

In the book *My Secret Garden,* there's an example which could be either fantasy or it could have really happened, of a woman who wrote about a guy stabbing a knife down between her legs into a table and telling her if she just relaxes she's not going to get hurt. Of course as long as that knife sits there she's going to be in fear. Meanwhile he proceeded to go down on her. It's possible that the combination of fear and turn-on are even more exciting than anything else. The woman went on to say that she returned to the fantasy of that rape afterward as an erotic daydream.

It could be that demonic possession of women, witches, and a whole range of supernatural things that we have attributed to women down through the ages grow out of the fact that certain women can be turned on while being punished at the same time. I'm suggesting that there are certain women who, when force and pain are combined with the visceral stimulation of their genitals, will have violent orgasms against their wishes. I should note that what I'm saying is pure speculation, based on extrapolation from literature, and from a few case histories that I've read in professional journals about sexuality.

Feminists contend that such ideas are born of male fantasy, that men want women to be like that, whereas in fact they aren't.

I think that radical feminists come up with glib answers and half-truths to everything that shows women as anything other than helpless victims. Feminists make the mistake of monolithically speaking of all women. This is a classic argument I've had with virtually every feminist I've known, who claims she is all women, and that all women are just like she is. All women are *not* alike. All men are not alike. Feminists simply respond out of prejudice, like any bigoted group. My argument with these women is that they generalize from their own feelings to all women, so that a woman who, for example, knows only her own orgasm, and what it feels like and how she gets it will then generalize to all women as to how clitorally orgasmic or vaginally orgasmic she should be. I have met women who are shocked and disgusted at the very thought of rape, even in fantasy, and are totally turned off to anything other than a gentle, loving, considerate man. I have also met women who are not turned on unless the man is rough and boorish, and I have slept with women who are most turned on when they are pinned down and held tightly.

If I wanted to find out more about what turns *men* on, I would ask women who've slept around a lot, or prostitutes, who are probably the greatest untapped resource in America for knowing what men's sexuality is *really* like! Xaviera Hollander has gotten rich from telling us what turns men on, and as far as I know, nobody has accused her of being a woman and, therefore, no authority on men. Conversely, a man who has slept with a large variety of women gets to see the commonalities and the differences among women, while any individual woman (who has not slept with any other women) only knows her own subjective reaction, which varies from woman to woman. Yet these women claim that it is pure arrogance for a man to suggest that perhaps he has some more knowledge about women's orgasm than a woman! . . .

There is a thin line between being forced to make the first move and rape. If a man is constantly put into the position, as our society's sexual mores do, of having to be the aggressor sexually, and of women having to say no initially, how does a man distinguish when she's actually saying no and when she is just doing what she thinks she's supposed to be doing? Although I'm not defending men's traditional reactions to rape (I hope), I can somewhat understand why men feel that rape victims really wanted it, if they perceive all women as wanting sex but feeling they should be saying no.

There's a significant number of men who have difficulty dealing with the idea that a woman is sexually free, now, but discriminating in who she will go to bed with. In 1956 I knew a girl who always had to tell men she didn't want to sleep with that she was a virgin, or else they wanted to know why she fucked for others and wouldn't fuck for them. These men seemed to feel in their heart of hearts that a woman's sexuality is for the servicing of men, and until this kind of misconception is brought out into the open, I think there will continue the kinds of sexist attitudes men have toward women's sexuality.

If a man looks into his unconscious, he'll probably see all kinds of negative feelings toward women. If he doesn't look into his unconscious, these negative feelings will be there and then he will form a vicarious identification with those men who are actually doing to women that which he is experiencing only in his unconscious. I think this is why we see so much rape in the media. If men are not in touch with their anger at women, they'll wind up perpetuating rape in subtle ways by supporting institutions and attitudes that are unsympathetic to women who have been raped, such as the whole police/judiciary system.

3
Rapist

"You look at these movies and think, 'Wow, I wonder what it would be like to go out and rape somebody!'"

Chuck

Regularly beaten by his stepmother and stepbrothers from the age of five, at thirteen he ran away from home and began a life of drug addiction and crime. At twenty, after two painful years of marriage, he separated from his wife and daughter, and felt enormous rage toward women for a year. One night while high on alcohol, pot, heroin, and downers, he went into a pornographic bookstore and watched a twenty-five-cent peep show that portrayed a man raping a woman. "It was," he said, "like somebody lit a fuse from my childhood on up. When that fuse got to the porn movie, I exploded. . . . It was like a little voice saying, "It's all right, it's all right, go ahead and rape and get your revenge; you'll never get caught." That night he attempted his first rape. Within ten days, he had attempted three, succeeded in one, and was contemplating a fourth. He spent six and a half years in a state hospital as a mentally disordered sex offender and has been out for a year. He is twenty-eight.

It is worth noting that while "Chuck" may represent a certain type of sex offender, many, perhaps most, rapists have psychological profiles that differ little from the "average man."

My real mom abandoned me when I was a baby. My first stepmom had three boys; from the time I was five they used to hold me and she used to punch me out for hours. I got beat three or four times a week by my stepmom—every time my dad was gone. I got tied up in my room for two days once. My job when I was younger was always to take care of the house. One time I didn't clean up the house, so they drug me stripped naked all through the living room on my back and I got first degree rug burns.

I couldn't eat meat fat as a kid and I refused to eat it. There was a time when my stepmom and two of her sons held me at the table and shoved a plate of fat in my face and made me lick the plate clean. I don't know why they were like that; 'cause I was the youngest, I guess. I used to go to school with big welts on my back from getting hit with a belt; I had black eyes, teeth missin'. Teachers used to see it and the law would let it go. My stepmom walked away a lot of times from child abuse cases. The one time I went to court as a kid, my grandmother begged the court to let her adopt me; the court said no because my father said I got my injuries somewhere else. He didn't want to lose me.

I hated my stepmom and my stepbrothers for beating me; I hated my real mom for abandoning me; I hated my dad for never standing up for me; I hated the laws; I hated the police.

I ran away from home when I was thirteen 'cause I couldn't take it no more. I just got tired of coming home and getting the shit kicked out of me. Up until I was thirteen, I was always pushed and shoved around. When I was thirteen, an uncle of mine who's now dead made a statement that if you back an animal into a corner, he's going to come out. At the age of thirteen, I started coming out, and the way I came out was violence. Every time I got into a fight with some dude or a family member, I always came out on top 'cause I learned how to street fight. I'd go for the kill.

It would be no just beatin' them up. I always tried to kill all the people I fought. You mess with me, you better kill me 'cause I'm going to do my damnedest to *kill* you, and if you *don't* kill me, you better watch your back 'cause I'll come back and I will kill you. From thirteen to twenty-one that's the way I believed.

My grandma gave me a few thousand dollars when I ran away from home. When that ran out I started workin' mowin' lawns, odd jobs, sleepin' on park benches, jumpin' freights, drivin' tractors or trucks. I learned how to drive a truck at sixteen. I was in and out of jail a lot for all kinds of things: theft, grand theft, drugs, drunk drivin', assault and battery, gang fights, street wars, concealing a deadly weapon, assaulting a police officer. . . .

I was into drugs at thirteen, dealing at sixteen, intertransporting at eighteen. By the time I was eighteen, I had a $200-a-day heroin habit and had to steal a lot to support it. I was strung out for seven years. I tried every branch of the armed forces and got turned down and that hurt. I wanted to go over to Vietnam and kill gooks and see what it felt like.

I got married when I was eighteen and that was okay at first; but then I found out my wife was bedding down with family members. I would get into bed with her; she'd just lay there and I'd get pissed off and go out and get drunk. One night I came home and caught my wife in bed with my cousin. I almost beat that boy to death. If it weren't for a black friend that was with me, I'd have killed him.

I started hating all women. I started seein' all women the same way, as users. I couldn't express my feelings to nobody. I'd go to work, clock in, and be by myself. I didn't trust anyone, not even the people I partied with. I had a bike and I rode with a lot of bikers, but I didn't talk to half of them. I went by different nicknames and nobody ever really knew me. I'd thought about murder and other ways of getting even with women and everyone who'd hurt me. I was just waiting to explode.

Then one night about a year after I split from my wife, I was out partyin' and drinkin' and smokin' pot. I'd shot up some heroin and done some downers and I went to a porno bookstore, put a quarter in a slot, and saw this porn movie. It was just a guy coming up from behind a girl and attacking her and raping her. That's when I started having rape fantasies. When I seen that movie, it was like somebody lit a fuse from my childhood on up. When that fuse got to the porn movie, I exploded. I just went for it, went out and raped. It was like a little voice saying, "It's all right, it's all right, go ahead and rape and get your revenge; you'll never get caught. Go out and rip off some girls. It's all right; they even make movies of it." The movie was just like a big picture stand with words on it saying go out and do it, everybody's doin' it, even the movies.

So I just went out that night and started lookin'. I went up to this women and grabbed her breast; then I got scared and ran. I went home and had the shakes real bad, and then I started likin' the feeling of getting even with all women.

The second one was at a college. I tried to talk to this girl and she gave me some off-the-wall story. I chased her into a bathroom and grabbed her and told her that if she screamed, I'd kill her. I had sex with her that lasted about five minutes. When I first attacked her I wasn't even turned on; I wanted to dominate her. When I saw her get scared and hurt, then I got turned on. I wanted her to feel like she'd been drug through mud. I wanted her to feel a lot of pain and not enjoy none of it. The more pain she felt, the higher I felt. As I did it to her, my head was back one night where my wife just lay there like a bump on a log and didn't show any pleasure. That's the one thing that was in my head. She was just layin' there doin' nothin'. It wasn't a victim no more; it was my wife.

I pulled out of her when I was about to come and I shot in her face and came all over her. It was like I pulled a gun and blew her brains out. That was my fantasy. She was the blonde that reminded me of my wife. In my head it was like poppin' caps off. I said, "Later," and just walked off and said, "Bye, Jane." That was my wife's name. The orgasm was a great thrill. In my head I blew Jane's brains out and that made it more of a thrill. I not only raped a girl or raped Jane in my head but I killed Jane. I killed her in my head and that was a beautiful high. When I blowed her away that day, she stayed dead for five years in my head.

It was the most beautiful high I'd ever experienced, better than any heroin I'd ever done. I was just floatin'. It didn't even feel like I was walkin' on the ground when I was walkin' home. I felt like a parachute was on my back and I was just hangin', floatin' in midair. I felt like I'd gotten even with different girls who'd fucked me over. I stayed floatin' until the next morning, and that's when I came down and I was sick, and then I wanted to get caught. I didn't know if she'd turned me in or not. I didn't know if they'd believe me if I said I'd done it. I got dressed and put the same clothes on and went lookin' for my next victim.

With my third victim, I ripped her clothes off and a man saw me and I just happened to turn around and saw him and I ran home. A week later when I was out lookin' for number four, I got busted. I'd had a lot of thoughts of committing suicide. When the cops busted me I had a gun on me and I was going to use the gun and shoot it out so they'd blow me away. I didn't care. I didn't have the heart to pull the trigger and kill myself. But I was killing myself and everything I remembered when I'd go out and rape. . . .

When I got caught a policeman called to me and I said, "Yes, I raped them three girls." When I was rapin' I was asking for help each time I raped—help or to be killed. I didn't trust anybody. In each of my attacks I wore the same clothes and I committed them a block away from each other. During the trial, the judge kept sayin', "We can send you to the hospital or we can send you to prison." I said, "Send me to prison, I don't care."

My sisters asked me why I raped and I told 'em I wanted to hurt you females in my family, just like I'd been hurt. They knew my real mom abandoned me and that my first stepmom beat the hell out of me all the time. And then I got married and she was bedding down all my family members. They understood, but they didn't want to believe it. They said you're just not that way. It took me three years to convince them that I *am* that way. The three girls I attacked represented to me my real mom, my stepmom, and my wife. They all had special features that reminded me of them.

In the hospital I was a loner at first. I kind of enjoyed feeling safe. I was in the best group therapy the hospital had to offer— what they call dry therapy. They sit around and hot-seat you, and for four years they couldn't get me to talk; they couldn't get me to open up. I'd go to staffing and they used to tell me, "If you don't start talking, we're going to ship your ass to prison." And I'd say, "Is that all you've got to say?" They'd say, "Yeah," and I'd say, "Start my paperwork, send me on my way."

We lived in dorms and after two and a half years, this guy sort of picked me out. We started talkin'. We started relatin' a lot. He showed me that everybody wasn't out to hurt me or use my feelings against me. He's the first dude I ever cried in front of. He told me, "Everybody's not out to hurt you, man. You're going to keep on the way you are, and you're just going to go nuts, and they're going to just blow your shit up."

I'd been there about four years the day he got out. He turned to me that day and he started cryin' and I was cryin', and he goes, "You can't let it beat you, man; you can't fight for the rest of your life, you'll always lose."

I sit around for about two months after that tryin' to understand what he was meanin' in what he said. It come to me: Why should I be a loser for the rest of my life? So I just started openin' up to people. I went to group one day and I said, "You know what? I've got to talk." I opened up for four hours worth of group that day. Everybody liked what I was puttin' out and saw that I was sincere in what I had to say.

A bunch of us were doin' drugs in the hospital and I told the people I was doin' drugs with, "I'm not going to spend the rest of my life in here. I want to go home." And I quit drugs. My friend wrote me a lot, tryin' to talk me into gettin' out and comin' to live in another state. I started makin' friends in group and started workin', started accepting other people's feelings, lettin' them know they could trust me. I call that place a hell-hole, and in some ways it is, but the help's there for people who want it.

MEN ON RAPE

When I went home I got harassed by the cops. They remembered me and ran drug tests and looked for track marks. They said, "We heard you was dead." I said, "No, I've just been away." I told them I was locked up for six and a half years and I'm not the same. They looked at me and said, "You don't seem the same anymore." I just grew up. That's all I did, I grew up.

If anything was to cause me to go back, it would be somebody messin' with my daughter. If anybody touches her I will definitely hurt 'em. That kid is my number one. She's my pride. I seen my daughter at Christmas for the first time in almost seven years. I'm supposed to get her this summer. She's got pictures of me all over her bedroom wall. She knows I'm her father. She sees me and she knows who I am.

When I was home I ran into a lot of people that I did drugs with who are still there. I told 'em, "If I ever find out that you turned my daughter on to drugs in any way I'm going to come back. You *know* I can find you." I told the cops, "If they ever turn my kid on to drugs, you better be ready for a war because that's how it is." I was strung out for seven years and I hate drugs. Drugs, rape, and child abuse are the things I hate most in life, because I've been through 'em. And I hate the law now because since I've been out I want to get into counseling, and they all say, "No, you don't have a license." I said, "I've got the best license in the world—I've been there," and they tell me you've gotta have a Ph.D. or umpteen years in college. . . . I'd like to work with kids. I'd like to keep kids from goin' through what I went through.

I've been out almost a year. At the hospital they had odds against me stayin' out this long. Just before I left they said, "We believe you won't rape, but we're puttin' odds that you'll go kill somebody." They don't think I'll rape again, but they think I'll pull a different crime.

Rape is sick. It hurts because that's what I was. I'm a rapist and I can say it. And I think that's what's going to help me stay out. I can look myself in the mirror and say, "You know what, you're a rapist." Or I can look in the mirror and say, "You ain't foolin' a motherfuckin' soul, man." I've looked in the mirror and talked to myself for hours since I been out. I say, "You ain't foolin' me. I know what's on your mind. I know what you are. I know what games you're playin', what you're not takin' care of." People come in and catch me and say, "You're sick"; but that's what's gonna keep me out. That's what's kept some of my other friends out.

My pants have got a chain and lock design on 'em. A friend asked me what that's for. I said, "It helps me remember. As long as I can remember, I ain't ever going back. When I can't remember, I'm going back." I've got my little family album with my release papers and my court transcript. I read through it once a week or so to help me remember and see what kind of a sick dog I was. It helps me want to fight. I've got my own ways. Even when I slip back, I've got ways of helpin' myself.

When I get pissed off or upset, I grab my handball and just work it out. I get to where I concentrate real hard on a picture of somebody I'm pissed at, and I just keep hitting it at that picture of the guy's face or girl's face—I keep hitting it 'til I can't move no more, 'til I'm physically and mentally drained. There's no one sending me back, not the state, not my old lady, not my family. They're not making me do another five, six, or seven years. I tell 'em, I say, "Hey, you ain't worth it, and I'll be goddamned if I'm going to spend another seven or eight years playin' your game. You can get out of my life."

If I'm hurtin' really bad inside I go talk to a friend because I know if I keep bottling it up, trippin' on it, fantasizing on it, I'm going to slip back into my old ways; I'm going to go out and hurt somebody. That scares the hell out of me. I call up my friends and say, "I gotta talk. This is what's goin' on—I'm going back to that old way of life. Talk to me, help me see my stop signs," and we just rap. Afterward, I feel better. I do different things, walk around and say "hi" to people, I even wave at cops. I just feel better after I talk to people. It's like everything's taken off my shoulders. That's all anybody ever really needs. I believe that. I could take you to the hospital and handpick as many people as you want who'll say the same thing as me. There are guys in there who really go nuts every time somebody commits a rape; they get fightin' mad. I seen 'em come close to jumpin' about half a dozen guys that come in that place for rape.

If there had been no pornographic movies showing rape, would you have raped?

I think I would've hurt a woman in a different way physically. If I wouldn't have committed rape I'd be in prison for murder right now, because it was goin' that way. I would've killed my next victim or the one after that. I would've killed somebody. I would've killed my stepmother, my mother, and my wife if I'd had the chance.

Pornographic movies have a lot to do with rape. I believe they shouldn't make movies of *any* kind of rape. They just shouldn't show it. Specials are okay because they can tell what can happen in rape, but a TV movie, a porn movie, or a regular movie about rape —they should ban them. You look at these movies and think, "Wow, I wonder what it would be like to go out and rape somebody!" I heard stories in the hospital of people saying society must condone it—they have it on TV and movies. I know five or six guys who saw pictures of rape in a dirty book and believed it was all right to go out and rape; just still snapshots and that justified it to them. It said, okay, go out and rape because it's in a dirty book; there's nothin' wrong with it. That goes for child molesting, too.

What could your victims have done to keep from being raped?

If they'd said, "Okay, go ahead, do anything you want," I don't believe I would've raped. If a girl had said, "Take me, I'm yours," I know I would've turned and walked away. It just wouldn't have been there for me. I didn't want somebody to be passive for me. I wanted somebody to show me the fear and the hurt that I always had to show. It was a turn-on to see em' scared and me being in control for once.

Rapists want to be in control. Somewhere in their life a woman destroyed their ego. Rape is a way a man rebuilds his ego, rebuilds his manhood. Shit like that.

I don't like what I did to those girls. If I seen a girl getting raped now I'd bust my ass tryin' to catch somebody's butt. I *know* that's the worst thing you can do to a female. I would probably hurt the man severely that raped a girl. I know I destroyed three lives in one way or another and it makes me *sick*. I have nightmares about it and I get freaked out because I get to tripping on it so hard. I know I can't go to my victims and say, "Hey, you know what? I wish I could turn back the hands of time, and know what I know now." That's a fantasy for me. That's bullshit. I wanta work against rape. I've seen the horror of it. I put my victims through hell and I know that women that's been raped get nothing but bullshit reasons and answers when they protest, and they don't need to hear that, 'cause it's not going to make 'em feel better.

When I was inside I worried about my sisters getting raped. I know what I'd want done to the man once he was inside. I got friends in all the prisons in this state, not just the hospital, and I know that wherever he went I could get that guy killed. I would have no remorse in doing it. I remember what my victims went through. I put my victims through a lot of hell. I know one that got a divorce. I feel bad about that. I know if her husband had gotten a hold of me, he would've killed me. I can understand that.

I got friends now that piss me off real bad. We'll be out partyin', and they'll see a girl on the street and say, "I'd like to rape her." I've gotten out of the car and told 'em, "You're a sick motherfucker! That's the worst thing you can do to a girl or a woman!" They don't know I've been in or what I've been in for. It totally freaks 'em out. I've lost a few friends that way.

Do you have more positive feelings toward women these days?

I admire the women nowadays. I think they've got just as much to offer as men do. I think the way they're going through life is really great. I believe in equal rights and all that stuff.

If I see a woman upset I'll go and ask her what's wrong, or if I see she needs help I'll be the first one to ask her. I don't like people hurt. I guess after six years in hospital I got all my hurt out.

I get scared sometimes around women. I see a nice-lookin' lady and I get to thinkin', man, I'd like to get her in the sack; man, I get scared and I get the hell away from her. When I'm walkin' out on the street at night and a girl passes me, I get scared. I'm afraid that after she passes me someone else will grab her, and she won't see his face but she'll remember mine. I have nightmares of raping again. I'm scared of doin' it again. The girls I rape in my nightmares are always the same ones that I did rape, so it's sort of a torment.

My stepmom now, my second stepmom, she's the best lady I ever met. To me she's my real mom. She gave me birth, in my eyes and in my heart and everything. I just love her to pieces. I'd hurt somebody if they ever hurt her. That's the way I am about her. She gave me something to look forward to. It made me see that women's not just bitches. Some out there are really beautiful and can give you love and respect if you have the right thing in mind. That's all she gave me, that's all I ever asked for. I just never got it when I was younger.

I had a girl friend for a few months and we just broke up two months ago. We used to talk about my rapes and my drug involvement and everything. She says, "It's hard to believe, you just don't seem that way." I got out my records and said, "Well, how good can you read?" She said, "What are you?" I said, "Well, I'm very violent, I'm an ex-junkie, I'm a rapist, and I've got human qualities, too. Those are just my bad qualities. I'm easy to hurt. I love people, I care about everybody. I don't like to see nobody hurt; I cry when I want to cry; when I want to be alone I'm alone. Mostly, I just love people."

She really hurt me. She just said, "I gotta be free. I gotta do what I gotta do," and that hurt 'cause I wanted to marry her. We're still friends. If she needs me I'm there in a flash. The hurt she did to me isn't the same as when the other women hurt me.

Are you able now to forgive people for what they do to you?

I've forgiven a lot of my family for what they did to me. I don't like it but I've forgiven them. Everybody has problems. The way I forgive is to say, "Hey, you've got problems, and I don't like what you did to me, but it's your problem and some day you'll deal with it, but I do forgive you." That's how I learned to forgive my dad for not bein' there when I needed him, how I learned to forgive my cousin who I caught in bed with my wife. I don't like what happened but I forgive him, and I forgive what my girl friend did to me. You'll always remember it and you'll have those feelings of being hurt, but you don't want to do anything about it.

Now there's people I won't forgive for the rest of my life, like my first stepmom and my real mom. It's gonna stay there. I can't forgive my mom for abandoning me when I was just a baby. I don't want nothin' to do with her. She was down here and I refused to see her. I don't ever want to see her.

I ran into my first stepmom one time when I was nineteen and I was walkin' through an alley and she ran up and grabbed me and hugged me. I said, "If you *ever* come around me, if you *ever* touch me, I'll kill you. I'll strangle you with my bare hands!" And I spit on her. If I found out she died today, I'd go down there just to spit on her, and hope one of her sons tried something.

It's like a scar that'll never heal. I pick at it when I see her. I don't want their friendship, their concern, nothin'. Yet, if I see 'em and when I see 'em, I want to always remember what they done to me, so I'll never do it to my kids. I've never hit my kid. As long as I remember what that lady and them boys did to me, there's no way. It's like the decal on my pants. It's a remembrance. The scar's a remembrance. My keepin' my own records is a remembrance. There are scars that I don't want to forget. As long as I don't, I'll be all right.

4

Husbands, Lovers, Friends

"I suddenly began to feel that I had *done* it, that *I* had somehow raped her."

Phil

Now twenty-five, when he was twenty-one his girl friend was raped. He grew up in New York and works in electronics.

We were both in school and were breaking up when she came back from vacation. We got together late in the afternoon and had a pretty good talk. I was feeling pretty distant and cool, and not knowing what I wanted really; she said she wanted to spend the night at my house. I said that I didn't want to, and she went home.

The next afternoon some friends dropped her off at my house. I said, "Hi, how are you doing?" and she replied in a real flat tone of voice, "I've got something I want to tell you; I was raped last night." I felt totally numb. I didn't feel anything except: something had happened that I'd had no experience of. I was trying to be concerned, even though I didn't really feel it, so I said, "What can I do?" It was confusing. She said, "Let me tell you what happened," also in a real flat tone of voice.

She'd gone home after leaving my house and gone to sleep. In the middle of the night somebody had come through her window, threatened her with a knife, and raped her. She was terrified and did what the guy asked—kept silent and went along with it. I asked if there was anything I could do and she said "No, not really." She knew she'd have a lot to get over and said she was going to go visit her parents.

Most of my feelings had to do with me. I felt inadequate and totally useless; I felt rejected because she was going away. I remember feeling that this was going to make her more distant and a lot more scared. I was also somewhat afraid for myself because I was living alone in a big house.

That night she stayed over and I wanted to make love to her. I knew she probably wouldn't want to, but I felt okay about asking. I was trying to be understanding and not pressure her and we wound up not making love.

I didn't feel anything for a couple of days; then I suddenly began to feel that I had *done* it, that *I* had somehow raped her. I spent weeks obsessing about it. It was a strange, disturbing feeling. I felt that there wasn't much difference between what the rapist had done with her and what I had done with her. The rapist threatened her with a knife, told her what to do, and she went along with it. When we had sex, I was in charge, and, in a sense, told her what to do and guided her. The similarity was in her passivity. I remember saying to friends, "The difference was *only* in consent!" And since the difference was only in consent I was almost as bad as the rapist.

I had a hard time feeling angry toward the rapist because I so *identified* with him. I couldn't get into the I-want-to-kill-him response because that felt like *I* was trying to kill *me*. I began to realize that, yes, I was on to something, but no, I'm obviously not a rapist, because consent makes all the difference in the world. I knew some women who were getting involved in rape work, and I asked them for some books to read. I read Diana Russell's *The Politics of Rape*, and found the book extraordinarily helpful. I started to see how rape wasn't just an isolated phenomenon, but was an extension of sex roles that get played out all the time. I would read accounts of women who'd been raped and get turned on, and feel so guilty I would want to kill myself. I slowly realized that men have been conditioned to find dominating and being aggressive erotic, and women conditioned to find being dominated and aggressed at, erotic.

Now, I want to acknowledge that conditioning and not deny it and make believe it's not true, but also make sure that it isn't used in any way to justify rape. I can accept my rape fantasies and even act them out with lovers.

What happened to your relationship?

The relationship ended. I didn't know how to relate to her being raped. I didn't know how to relate to her needing a whole lot. A lot of the dynamics of my relationships with women focused on *my* needs. I was almost expecting her to meet my needs and take care of herself, and she was too smart to do that.

"It was like she had stuck a knife in my stomach and she was carelessly cutting my guts out."

Gary

A thirty-year-old civil engineer and architect who sculpts, he recently found himself breaking up with a woman after she was raped. He is a Vietnam vet.

We had been together for two years and things were gradually falling apart. Sheila was getting fervently involved with an environmental group and I disagreed with some of her opinions and attitudes. She'd just had an abortion and there was a lot of tension between us over that. It seemed as if she withdrew completely from me and made the decision herself. I felt that my voice wasn't really heard. All my reasons for having the abortion were falling away, and I felt, and still feel, hurt and ripped off by the abortion.

When she left on a camping trip in the Sierras, we didn't even kiss each other good-bye. But she called me as soon as she got out of the mountains, and there was a really good feeling between us, and she said she wished I'd been there, and I told her to call me back later and I'd fly out and come back with her, and now I really wish I had.

The day she was due back she called me and said she'd be at the transit station at midnight. She sounded kind of strange, but I figured she was just tired or worn out from traveling. I went and picked her up and she seemed distant and strange, and we came home and she talked in a cheerful way about some of the things she'd done, and she and I were in the kitchen alone, and she said, "I've just got to tell someone I know," and I thought, "Oh, Jesus, I don't think I'm gonna like this, and I thought she was gonna tell me she was in love with somebody," and she says, "I was raped tonight," and it was like the roof fell in on me, I went into shock, I couldn't talk. I was making absolutely no contact. She went on and told a few details about it, and it was like she was killing me and didn't realize it. It was like she had stuck a knife in my stomach and she was carelessly cutting my guts out.

To know the inside of a woman sexually is a way of knowing someone that is incredibly intimate and personal, and I knew Sheila that way. It's some of the deepest knowledge that I know of, and somehow I felt inside of her, violated, forced, and it was the most awful, horrible, *wrong* feeling I've ever felt. It was killing me, doubling me up. Finally, I managed to say, "Listen, I can't hear this anymore right now. I'll be right back. I gotta leave," and I came upstairs, and I walked into my friend Edward's room, sat down on his bed, and I just collapsed and went into hysterics. I couldn't even talk to him. I just cried and cried and cried, and he couldn't figure out what had happened, and after about five minutes I was able to talk and I said, "She's been raped!" and he thought I said, "She's *being* raped!" and he started running around in circles, and it took me awhile to say some more, and I said, "Please, please go down there and be with her, but don't leave her alone, I can't do anything now," and he went down and I cried some more and got myself together after about ten minutes and went downstairs, and they were talking about flowers or something, and I thought "What's going on here?" and Edward left and she said, "I didn't want you to tell him. I don't want him to know. I don't want anybody to know." I said, "What do you mean you don't want anyone to know? That's what you love people for, to help you when you need help." When you really need help and somebody else loves you, it's one of the most beautiful things you can do for them, to let them help.

We slept together that night and it was one of the warmest, tenderest nights I can remember. All night long her body was moving and moaning and aching and I held her and my physical presence was, I felt, comforting her, and she was very, very comforting to me. I needed to be with her so much. I needed to comfort her so much.

The next day she started talking about going to see her parents in Canada. Right from the first I said, "That's a bad idea, I don't like that idea. You can't just come back here and drop something like this on me and leave me. I know it happened to you but it happened to me, too. I'm alive, I'm feeling. These things are going on inside of me, it's killing me, you can't leave me." And she just went right along and made plans to go to Canada and that afternoon I took her to the hospital, and we spent an afternoon in the hospital that was very, very tender, warm, and beautiful. It was one of the most painful and one of the most beautiful days of my life, and we came home and I asked her to marry me, which I'd done before, and I got next to belligerent about it. I said, "Listen, you've got to marry me, this can't go on, I've got to find some fuckin' shelter from this, it's too heavy."

I guess I was asking her to share the responsibility of the love and she got pretty upset and said, "No, I'm not gonna marry you." I realize now it was really a bad time for me to be saying that, but I also realize it was a bad time for me, too.

I really, really needed to give her something that would make it better. I didn't mean I could take the rape away, or erase it, or pat her on the head and make it all go away, but I really needed to share in her pain and in her love.

She went ahead and said she was going to go to Canada, which I didn't like. I acted poorly. I told her that I thought she was being really unfair, really cruel to leave me then. I took her to the airport and let her go with an air of estrangement.

I came back here and she called and she was crying, nearly in hysterics. She decided not to go because the plane was a DC-10 and there had been accidents with DC-10s recently. I ran off to get her and told her I'd been an asshole and apologized, and we came home and went to bed that night, and it was another night of being warm and close and we made love that night, I don't know how or why.

The next day she leaves for Canada and comes back two weeks later and doesn't have any time for me, and we go through another scene, and all I could do was sit and ache. A few days later I said to her, "I don't think you care very much for me. You have time for everybody but me."

She said, "You're right. I don't think I love you. I don't think I ever loved you. You realize you made love to me two days after I was raped! You realize how that made me feel! Another dick inside me! Another cock!"

Goddamn, that surprised the hell out of me! I had no idea she felt that way. I'd always told her not to make love if she didn't want to. In fact, I've gotten angry at her at times when I felt she was making love to me because I wanted to. She told me that she made love to me because I was upset, and she felt she had to do something. That made me feel as awful as anything I've ever felt.

What was going on in my head was that she needed to make love in a positive way, and maybe the sooner the better. I told a friend a few days later that we'd made love and his reaction was,

"I'm so glad to hear that, I was really worried because so often a woman feels unclean and that her lover doesn't want anything to do with her." We had no connection as to what we were doing. She was making love out of a sense of responsibility to me, and I was making love because I wanted to ease her pain.

We ended that conversation with an understanding that we had broken up, and that if we needed to talk we could call each other. There were four or five phone calls in the next few weeks, and I was feeling worse and worse and she was getting more militantly feminist.

Then one day she called and said, "Guess what. If we hadn't had that abortion, I would have had a child today." I threw the phone on the floor and started crying and went damn near crazy. I had so many different emotions flying around in my head. I hated her for saying that. Suddenly I had the rape and the abortion and the breakup to deal with all at once, and for her to say that in an easy lighthearted way struck me as incredibly insensitive and cruel.

A few weeks later I was getting used to having a cloud over my life and feeling really diminished, when I got a letter from Sheila, who was now in Trinidad, and she invited me to come down and visit her, and she talked about how the society drives women crazy down there, and in the States, and everywhere, and she said she mourns for all those women caught in this cultural quagmire, and she said, "I mourn for you." It was very poignant and brought me up.

When Sheila was raped, what exactly was the feeling that went through you?

It was like *I'd* been violated. That deep, sexual knowledge I talked about. You just can't *know* anybody, can't *touch* anybody more deeply than that. Through that knowledge, I had a knowledge of the violation, and felt deeply connected to it. That feeling lives in a very deep place in me. I was hurt there very, very much. It wasn't a feeling that my property had been abused or used. It wasn't a selfish feeling. Through that feeling, my attitude and ideas about rape have really changed. Now, if I were near the scene of a rape, I'm afraid I'd kill somebody.

I spent three days really uncertain whether I could live and stay sane without trying to kill the rapist. Not for vengeance, although I wouldn't have minded a little vengeance. The thing that was really bothering me was that this guy was crazy, that he was way outside of my understanding of humanity, and that at any time he could decide that she liked what happened, and that she would want some more. He knew her name and address, he could decide that she was too great a risk to let live. I wasn't sure I could live with that much fear. *I* had done nothing. *She* had done nothing. This motherfucker had done all that. He put us in that position. Why do I have to swallow that? Why does she have to swallow that? . . . The reason I finally didn't kill him, or try to kill him, or whatever, was that I realized I could never be absolutely sure who he was.

The virtue of the court system and due process is that you've gone through as thorough an examination as you can, and you're sharing the responsibility as carefully as you can with other people, and you're saying that this man did this act and must suffer for it. That would be an incredible responsibility to take on: to be judge, jury, and executioner.

I had plots against this man. Do you take him out and cut his legs off? Do you cut his balls off? Do you blind him and cut out his tongue? What do you do? Do you sneak up behind him and shoot him behind the ear? What do you do? I called my brother, who I felt understood what I was going through, and he said, "Just tell me who he is. I know some people who'll break both his legs for two hundred dollars." I said "Oh, fuck, I don't want anything to do with people like that. It's the same thing!" My brother offered to help me. At that point it was kind of getting into "the family's been wronged and we're going to get on our horses and ride out there and kill the motherfuckers."

What was really motivating me in these violent fantasies toward the rapist was a sense of fairness. He had done an indescribably violent act and now he had left two innocent people in fear that he might do another, and I felt perfectly justified in saying we don't have to live in that fear.

What did the rape do to Sheila?

I feel the rape has moved Sheila incredibly toward self-hatred, self-abuse, and self-destruction. She has swallowed her guilt, the responsibility for it. She *knows* she's not responsible for it, yet she *feels* responsible somehow. The words fall apart around this one. She's swallowed something ugly that's stuck in her, and the way to regurgitate it is to scream and cry and collapse on the floor and get it out, just feel it, and let it out of you.

That's a terrible price to pay, to be deeply poisoned in the deepest part of yourself, in your love, and to have something inside you which you need to feel, but which is horrible to feel.

What is the greatest harm done to women by rape?

The greatest amount of harm done collectively is in the fear and the tension, that closing of an openness toward other people. It doesn't even have anything to do with sexuality. The fear of rape casts a whole shadow on the richness and warmth of human culture.

I can't really begin to understand why a man rapes. I can project myself into it in a certain way to a certain extent, but I can't really imagine it. There've been times when I've read newspaper articles about rape and the thing that is titillating or attractive to me is the idea of pure sexual satisfaction. I don't have to talk someone into it, or beg or borrow, there's no game being played. It's just a direct immediate satisfaction of my needs.

What was your experience of rape in Vietnam?

The one incident I heard about involved a twelve-year-old girl being passed around through a platoon. The idea of it sickened me.

My experience in Vietnam was unique because I lived with the Vietnamese, was isolated from Americans and had gone through six months of language school and Vietnamese culture and traditions training and I knew something about what to expect. The main attitude I came across among Americans was an incredible amount of racism. The Vietnamese were generally looked upon as lesser beings. They were considered stupid, cowardly, small, ugly, poor, to be killed if you wanted to. I'm sure sexual attitudes toward the women went right along with this, and that rape occurred. Some soldiers had this attitude that they could go into a hamlet or village and take what they wanted and slap people around. Rape in Vietnam would have to be seen in the larger context of hatred and disrespect for the Vietnamese.

"Rape was one of the things that drove me out of New York."

Stavros

A thirty-three-year-old psychotherapist, he has intervened in no fewer than four attempted rapes, including one on his wife.

I was sitting at home one night when I heard a scream coming from about a block away. I always keep my eyes and ears open at night, and if I hear screaming I usually do something about it. I jumped up and recognized it was my wife's voice, so I ran into the kitchen, picked up a kitchen knife, and ran out the door. We lived on a hill and I ran down the hill, and saw my wife turning the corner, running up the hill screaming in an obvious state of panic. As she came up she blurted out that somebody had tried to rape her, and at that point I interrupted her and brought her back to the house and went after him running down the street. To do what I don't know. I just felt a combination of fear and rage. By the time I'd gotten down the hill he'd taken off.

I came back to the house and calmed her down and held her, and asked her what happened. She'd gotten a ride hitchhiking and the guy seemed to be okay. She got in the car and they took off, and when they got to the corner where our house was she said, "Well, this is where I want to be let off," and he grabbed her around the neck, and pulled her down and stepped on the accelerator, at which point she, of course, freaked out, but had enough presence of mind to reach up and pull him by the hair and kick open the door. He had to put on the brakes at least temporarily; she ran out and hit the sidewalk, and this guy started to back up after her, at which point she screamed and I came running down.

The cops came and she tried to describe this guy, and the way she was describing him, it was me. If I were walking down the street, and the cops got this description, it would've been me, which is very striking on a number of levels.

For a few months afterward, Susan, my wife, was very scared of walking down onto the streets. I had another reaction. I had this tremendous sense of rage, more than I've ever felt in my life, and I kept having this image of getting this guy. I wanted to catch him and cut his balls off. It was a very primitive feeling. I know my own anger, but this was something different. For the first time in my life, I knew I had the capability of killing somebody. I had never admitted that to myself. I think that if I'd caught the guy, I would've done my best to kill him, and of course I didn't, so I was stuck with all this rage.

For about six months, I walked around like a time bomb. I felt *tremendous* rage. I was obsessive about it. I would sit down and try to analyze what was going on and there were several things that came out of it. One was a strong protective feeling toward Susan, my wife. Second, not only was there a potential threat of her being violated, but of me being violated through her. Practically speaking, the fear that she felt also lessened the amount of intimacy she was capable of having with me. I had this enormous rage, not only for the would-be rapist, but toward any man who showed aggressive tendencies toward women. And, of course, having had psychological training, I realized that some of this had to be projection, that I was looking not only at this guy, but at the rapist inside of me. So I looked more and more closely at what that's about and it took me into Greek myths. I started looking into the myth of Demeter and Persephone and Hades. It's what Jung would call an archetypal myth of rape. It's about a god from the underworld who comes up to the surface and abducts this young ethereal maiden named Persephone, who's the daughter of Mother Earth, and carries her into the underworld, and rapes her, and marries her in the depths of the underworld. I began identifying with the myths very closely. I started looking at how I needed women for something other than simple intimacy. I got more in touch with the user in me, the aggressor in me, the one who wants to drag women down into the underworld.

The attempted rape, which felt like a rape to me in that *I* felt raped, forced me to examine all this. It wasn't a feeling that my property had been damaged. I come from a Greek background so there was a sense that my honor was at stake, though it goes much deeper than the word "honor" suggests. It was like the softest side of me was being fucked with, because she was the soft side of me. I felt violated, my psyche felt violated, my feminine side felt violated. It tied into some of my own fears because I've always imagined that the softer I became the more vulnerable I would be to attack. That hasn't proven to be true. The softer I've become, the less vulnerable I've become. Ten years ago when I first started softening, quite often people would misrepresent that as homosexuality or effeminacy, and I would be attacked verbally or physically. So the attempted rape spotlighted my own struggle about being a man and being soft.

I blamed myself to some degree because three months before that incident my wife and I had been living with a roommate, a man, and we decided to move out, and we were all sitting in the living room and we broke the news to him and he flipped out and jumped up and grabbed her because she was, in a sense, provoking him, she was tongue-lashing him, and before I could do anything about it, he had thrown her across the room and broken her nose. This was a close friend and I went into shock and couldn't believe that he would physically violate her. She went running out of the room. He and I squared off to fight and I realized that this was my closest male friend and we cooled off.

After the incident with my friend, I started condemning myself for my lack of physical strength, for my lack of acknowledgment that women are physically weaker and more available as targets, and that when I'm with a woman it's natural for me to be prepared to protect her. As a child I was taught that you never ever get close to hurting women physically. It's your duty to be protective toward all women. Even a subtle form of aggression is frowned on. Underneath this gallant, courteous attitude toward women is a lot of anger at women because they have tremendous emotional power, especially if you're denying your own feelings and relying on women, in some sense, to teach you to feel.

Where does your own sexual rage come from?

The fear of impotence, of being not only needy but helpless to fulfill that need, is the closest I can get to the source of my own sexual rage. Needing to let go to a woman and at the same time feeling frustration in not being able to let go, because in the past I haven't been able to, and also because some women have been socialized to see that as weakness and to exploit it.

Although I've never had rape fantasies, I've certainly felt the aggression in me when I'm fucking, as opposed to making love, particularly with women whom I perceive are not fully available to me, and what that is, of course, is a projection of *me* not being fully available to me. And then I find myself fucking them, trying to get deeper and deeper inside, and that comes close to a rape fantasy. I've been scared of letting that out. When I feel rage I get away from the woman. I've never gotten to the point where I'm feeling a blind rage. It's usually a little colder and subtler than that. It poses as a sense of distance and control, objectifying and controlling the other person and using her as an instrument.

Did the attempted rape affect your sexual feeling toward your wife?

No, the only thing that interrupted it was my own rage,

which fortunately didn't go toward her. I felt protective and sad toward my wife. She was not very alert on the street, she was an innocent, and of course innocence attracts its opposite. So I was very frightened for her, and whenever we would walk in a bad neighborhood I would get very protective toward her and try to rope her in.

Did you resent having to be more protective toward her?

Yes, and I resented her to some degree. After the incident with my roommate she said that she didn't trust my reaction. I felt emasculated. I thought, "My God, if the woman I'm closest to can't trust my reaction, how can I? Am I really prepared to protect her?" The attempted rape called all this into question and she rubbed it in. I felt guilt and resentment toward her, which in turn made me even angrier at the person who attempted to rape her. I started studying martial arts, which I've continued to study and which has helped me get out a lot of rage and feel more at peace with myself.

The attempted rape threw me back on a very old image of what it means to be a man, at least in Greek culture. First of all, in terms of physical capability, I became not only more protective toward Susan, but more domineering. I don't think you can become more protective without becoming more domineering. I also became more of a father toward her. I had quite a lot of fear out on the street that I was working through when the attempted rape occurred, so I had to confront both my own and her fear, which was quite a burden.

What other experiences of rape have you had?

Rape was one of the things that drove me out of New York. I was getting scared for my own survival. Either I would have to stop listening to the screams at night or I would have to get out of there.

Just before I left New York, I personally intervened in three attempted rapes in one month. In one month! In each case I suspended my own better caution and went after them. Once on

Third Street I heard screams from a tenement building and I grabbed a bar off a police lock and paused for a minute to think twice about putting myself in danger and realized, no, I've got to do this, and I grabbed the bar and went downstairs. He had just left and he'd had a gun. The second time in my own building, it was right outside my door. I kept an ice pick by the door and I grabbed the bar and opened the door and saw him running down the stairs and went after him. God knows what would've happened if I'd caught up with him. I probably would've gotten hurt myself. Somebody else on the first floor went after him and tackled him and the police took him away. The third time was again in my building on the Lower East Side. A woman came down from the rooftop bloody.

"I think forgiveness is something that has to happen to make that experience finally over."

Alex

He is thirty-one, six feet six, gay, and a part-time graduate student in creative writing. His closest woman friend was raped, and her recent retelling of the experience evoked many new perceptions.

Susan came suddenly to visit me from New York a few days ago. The bulk of her visit was her telling me about an incident that happened a little over a year ago in which she was threatened with a knife and tied up and raped. We sat up all hours of the night and she talked and talked about all her feelings about what happened to her. She said it was the first time she really felt comfortable talking about it with a man. There were a couple of times when she was shaking and she said, "Do you know what it means to me to sit here talking to a very large man like you with the door locked late at night, even though I know you're my friend and I know you won't hurt me?"

During her visit something got tapped in me; since she left, that's about all I've been talking about. It forced me to encounter a whole lot of feelings I get projected at me because of my size and the way I appear to women and the kind of fear I generate in them. That fear irks me but I understand it a lot better now. A woman will get on an elevator and look at me suspiciously and even though she's going to the eighth floor she'll push four and six just in case. What am I supposed to do? Turn to her and say it's all right or something? That would just freak her out. So I just stand there and go through this whole number. I want to go, "Look, I have seven sisters and I'm not into women anyway, so what's the big deal?" I understand their caution much better now. It's not being fearful; it's just being cautious. I used to look at it as, "This is a pain and why are they projecting that on me?"

Just the other evening I was walking home and about a block away I could see this young girl waiting for someone out on her stoop. Then she saw me coming and I could sense her going through a little act of stepping very slowly back inside, behind the door. I passed by and then looked back and she was stepping back outside again. I shouldn't feel angry about that. I should feel bad that it has to be that way. I respect her paranoia and understand it more now.

In New York on a subway, there have been times where women will size up a situation and purposely sit next to me and act as if they're with me. Sometimes there'll be just a few people scattered on a subway train and the doors will open and a couple of unsavory people will get on, and a woman will get up and come sit next to me because she's made all the choices and decided, "I worry about him the least."

I come from a large family with seven sisters, and rape was sort of an unnamed theme that ran through our house. My mother was always saying to my sisters, "You *don't* ride with strangers, you *don't* do this, you *don't* do that"; but she would never use the word "rape." Because I was male and the oldest, I was responsible for seeing that nothing happened. I was constantly told, "You've gotta watch your sisters. God, what would your father say if anything happened?" I don't think any of my sisters have ever been raped. I think I would know if they had, but there have been isolated instances where each one of them came home crying that some man grabbed them on the breast or something. My oldest sister had a couple of bad experiences hitchhiking. She jumped from a car stopped at a red light once; another time she talked her way out of getting raped by telling the guy she was having her period. I always felt bad for my sisters, but my general attitude was, "You can get run over by a car, you can get pickpocketed on the bus, or you can get raped."

I don't think my mother's been raped, though she certainly hinted at the little rapes that occurred in relation to my father. My father traveled a couple of weeks every month. We were Catholics, so my mother saw it as her moral duty for those two weeks, whether she wanted to or not, to have intercourse. There were plenty of times when we were all very aware that she wasn't in the mood and would show a kind of hesitancy. It was something we could feel. She was doing her duty. As I got older and thought about rape and what it means, I could see how she *was* raped in a way. It *was* against her will. It's rape with a lower case "r." She thought of it as her duty to have sex just as it was his duty to provide. She was always a good Catholic; she had ten kids and three miscarriages. I don't think she was a very sexual person really. . . .

Did you feel angry at the man who raped your friend?

I don't feel angry at the guy. I feel mostly concern for her and a lot of interest about how she's working it out. One of the things we talked about that made her very mad and made her get up and leave the room and tell me I had to stop this was when I started talking about forgiveness. In retrospect I probably shouldn't have brought it up. It made her the most angry when I was talking about her inability to see him as a person. I've had a lot of conflicting feelings about people who have violated me and hurt me, and when I get right down to it there's a key in being able to forgive them. I think that's viable. I'm not trying to diminish her experience or her anger or anything else; I'm just trying to hint at a way she can confront some of this better.

I think forgiveness is something that has to happen to make that experience finally over. Even though it was a horrible violent encounter, it was an encounter. It's like falling in love and being open and vulnerable and getting fucked over and feeling violated and robbed. Afterward you feel helpless and don't know what to do about it. When that happens you give a lot of power to the person who fucked you over. In that sense, that nineteen-year-old kid who raped her and who's now in prison a thousand miles away still has a lot of power over her. There's still someone I haven't seen for a while who I was in love with who's gone and over, and I've invested him with a lot of power, and that's where the forgiveness comes in. The forgiveness is taking back the power. Forgiveness is one of the keys, the realization that it's just another person over there. It's just this nineteen-year-old kid who raped me. It's not being afraid of the dark, or every man in every vestibule, or every man in the street who looks at me sideways.

To the rapist, she was a nonperson, and now he's a nonperson to her, and she wants the death penalty for him. She gets a lot of pleasure out of the fantasy that in prison he'll get raped over and over and over. That makes her feel good. That's where forgiveness comes in: evil gets passed on and eventually somebody gets it and is strong enough not to pass it on.

5
Lawyers

"If I could get my client off by appealing to the jury's sexism I probably would."

Bill

He is a public defender whose job it is to defend people who cannot otherwise afford a lawyer. He has taken four rape cases to trial and in each case his client was acquitted—twice to his amazement—as a verdict of guilty seemed so obvious to him. Not long after one of the trials, the woman he lives with was raped. He is forty.

I don't care whether my client is guilty—I never have. The truth is irrelevant to me. You're the county, you hire me and pay me forty thousand dollars a year to defend people to the best of my ability. That's what the bar association says I'm supposed to do. If I don't do that I'm taking their money under false pretenses. Sometimes people get on the witness stand and I think they're lying, and I don't care, because I don't care whether they did it or not.

The state in all of its power, with the police, and the courts, and the district attorney, is going to try to put this man in prison, and try to prove that he committed a crime. My job is to see if there is sufficient room to raise a reasonable doubt as to whether he did it or not. One of the things that makes it a little easier is a case I had when I was very new as an attorney. I had a client who was accused of assaulting someone with a gun. He was a little weasely, ratty-looking guy with greasy hair and bad skin. He just *looked* unpleasant. He told me his side of the story; it wasn't very believable and I had heard a lot of stories. And I said, "Listen, I'm going to take this case to court because that's what you want. They've offered you thirty days in the county jail and probation. If you lose this in court you're looking at at least a year. Now, if you want to go to trial with that story, I'll fight like a dog for you." And that's true: I don't like to lose, because at some point my ego gets involved. I tell this to my clients because some of them think their attorney doesn't like them. And they understand at some basic level that they don't even count. When the case goes to trial it's combat between two people and they're just tools.

The point of the story is that midway through the trial it turned out that my client was telling the truth and I couldn't believe it: it shook me up. That was the dumbest, hokiest story I'd ever heard in my life, and it was absolutely true, verbatim.

In terms of rape, not every man who's charged with rape is guilty, and it's not for me to make these judgments. In my job as a public defender, I don't get to pick and choose my clients. Most people who are accused of crimes are poor; those who wind up in the public defender's office are the poorest of the poor and have no place else to turn.

In all the rape cases I've had, the man denied that it was rape, and claimed the woman consented. I don't get to see the victim for a long time; and in the course of that time I get to talk to a *person*—he doesn't foam at the mouth; there's no blood coming off his fingers. Politically, most of the people who commit rape are in the same socioeconomic class as most of the people who commit other crimes. And there's a kind of rage that I see in rape cases that's born out of the same oppression that makes people rob stores and violently injure people. And I can see a person who in this society is so oppressed and downtrodden that rape becomes just a way of being powerful, so he rapes someone, not even knowing or caring who that person is, just to have power over them.

No one ever addresses the issue of what happened to this guy for the past twenty-five years. They address what he did that day. So in some larger sense I really don't care about what he did, and I'm not totally comfortable with that, because I know the victim didn't do anything to him either.

I think women are oppressed and rape is part of the reason. If all the energy women put into catching rapists were put into reforming a system that produces rapists, that would be more legitimate to me—although I don't expect people to just take it from me. Women want to go after the rapist because he's the one that hurts them personally. I just think that in some sense it's bigger than that.

I've had clients who were mentally disordered, and all their crimes involved sexually assaultive behavior toward women. With one client, it moved from violence to economic crime, but it all included sexual assaults on women. He's got a bad problem. They're not going to deal with his problem in prison; that won't do any good. They're going to punish him? My opinion when I look at someone like that is that his *life* is a punishment. Perhaps if I were a woman, or I were raped, I'd feel differently. Women have every reason to feel enraged.

The first time I saw a D.A. question a rape victim he appeared to be sexually excited; he was breathing heavily and his voice was very quiet. He could've asked her if she was wearing underwear, and if the rapist removed the underwear. Instead he said, "Did you have on panties? Did he tear off your panties?" "Panties" to me is an erotic word. He looked obviously excited, and it was *his* witness. He was supposed to be defending her from any brutalities the system might visit upon her.

I want rape to stop, but I don't want rapists to be prosecuted, because that's just stupid. Until somebody does something about the socioeconomic causes of most crime, I'm not going to look at somebody who commits a crime and say, "You're bad." I've been robbed, burglarized, my car's been stolen four times, and no one's ever been put in jail for it and no one will be.

How do you feel about the man who raped your lady friend?

If I knew who raped and beat up my lady friend, I don't think I'd call the police. It would be personal and I would go after him and bash his skull in. It's not related to what I do in a courtroom because in a courtroom I have a job to do, and the job is very specific: to defend my client to the best of my ability. That may seem slightly schizophrenic, but it's a slightly schizophrenic world. . . .

In two of the four rape cases I've taken to court, I was shocked that the jury found my client not guilty—I even felt slightly indignant. I thought it was blatantly obvious my client was guilty. In one trial, the woman was hitchhiking and I think that was why the jury acquitted. They wanted to know why she was hitchhiking. What was she doing there? She was hitchhiking, she needed a ride! She didn't say, "Hey, rape me." Give her a break.

In the other case, a prostitute was physically very torn up and the jury spat on her because she was poor and a prostitute. No one cared. That's the same oppression my clients get. After those cases I stopped talking to jurors about why they didn't find him guilty.

In many courtrooms in the U.S., whites have been acquitted in crimes against blacks because of appeals to the racism of the jury. I assume you find that morally repugnant. Analogously, many rapists have gotten off because of sexist appeals to the jury. Do you want to get your client off because you've raised a reasonable doubt about his guilt, or because of the prejudices against women that exist in this society? Where is the bottom line?

The bottom line is in getting my client off. If I saw myself appealing to the jury's sexism I would probably wonder about it and, it's true, I don't look at it as harshly as appealing to the jury's racism. The effect of the women's movement on me has been as strong as on anyone else, but I'm no one special; I try to win my cases. If I could get my client off by appealing to the jury's sexism I probably would, because I'd be more concerned with this one guy and his freedom than the ethical issue of sexism. If I didn't appeal to their sexism and I thought I could've to get my client off, and he went to prison, I probably would feel pretty bad about it. In the heat of the battle I probably pull out a lot of stops and I may have appealed to the jury's sexism without even real- izing it.

Are you ever rough on rape victims during cross-examination?

I do not brutalize unless I see them lying. If I see them lying about anything, I say wait a minute, is this guy telling the truth? I mean he *didn't* do it; maybe this *was* consent. What's going on? If I see an opening or a contradiction, I develop it as much as I can. If you committed a crime and you're guilty, would you feel that your lawyer was morally right in laying off the victim, being nice to her because you're guilty, not defending you, not trying every way that he can to get you off? If you're defending a man accused of rape and he doesn't admit the crime, to be nice to a rape victim on the stand is to prejudge the case. If my client is telling the truth, then *he's* the victim and not the woman.

When your lady friend was raped, did you feel any guilt about having defended rapists?

No, I didn't. This is my job; everybody expects me to try to get my client off. I've always thought of rape as an ugly crime, but I've defended people who had allegedly slashed people with knives, and blinded them, and killed people; so in the sense that rape is an ugly crime, it isn't as ugly as death. The woman I live with was raped; I'm glad she wasn't killed. I'd prefer that she be raped than killed. She probably would feel right now that they'd have to kill her the next time. So maybe from her point of view death is not as bad as rape.

What did you go through with her when she was raped?

We had just started seeing each other. I really loved her and this is the monkey wrench of all time: a man and a woman in a developing relationship, and the woman gets raped. I was petrified. I didn't know whether being with her during this time would make it impossible to continue seeing her on a romantic and sexual basis or not. Sex I was willing to forego as long as it took. I felt no less of a sexual attraction, but I felt less of a sexual urge, because I was afraid to be sexual in her presence. I was afraid I'd scare her. I didn't want sex and me to be associated with each other, because rape is sex somehow, and I didn't want to be a part of it—didn't want her to see me as somehow one of *them*. I wanted to disappear because I didn't know what I could do. I was very supportive and I know she knows that. I was there for five or six days and I just took care of her like she was two years old. I'm very intuitive and I felt fine about taking care of her, but a month later I didn't know what to do. She couldn't relate to me because she was too busy relating to the fact that she'd been brutalized. But since that wasn't always apparent, she just got confused. *I* felt brutalized in a way. I could empathize so strongly I would quake.

After she was raped, I asked to be taken off rape cases for a while. I wanted to be able to talk about my work and it would've been difficult if I was defending rapists. I've gotten back on rape cases since then and it hasn't been a problem.

What did your friend's rape teach you about the effects of rape on women?

The extent of the damage. I used to think that it was the penetration, the violation of your privates, that made the crime so hideous; but I don't believe that now. I think the greatest horror of it is to be out of control of your life for half an hour; to not know whether you're going to come out of it alive can so rip your identity that it's hard to come out of it in one piece. For most of the women I've talked to, the sex is irrelevant. They're not there when the intercourse is taking place; they're somewhere in the back of their mind. I think of the number of women who've had intercourse with me who didn't really feel like it, but it's two o'clock in the morning and they say "what the hell," and give in, and just escape somewhere. But to be out of control of your life for a period of time is another matter.

The doors get locked a lot now. My lady's afraid to come home when I'm not there. Someone once came into our house when we were gone and she began to shake. This was two years later. I see more clearly now both the extent of the damage and wherein the damage lies.

Right after my friend was raped she moved up on a hill to the second floor of a two-story apartment and about five months later we were walking down the stairs and she just glanced up; I knew it had something to do with the rape: she was looking up to see how far she would have to jump if it happened again. She'd risk at least breaking a lot of bones rather than be raped. She's in a little better position maybe than a lot of women who were raped, because she fought back; she bit the guy's finger to the bone, and she kicked him in the head. He broke her nose and punched her out, and finally she just gave.

Now my lady is becoming an expert in karate. I hope she meets the guy that did it, but I hope that when she meets him, that it *is* him. Good luck to him. He deserves what he'd get. I don't know that he deserves to go to prison, because that's stupid.

I didn't get into this line of work because I wanted to defend rapists. I got into it partly out of the recognition that poverty is determinative at every step of the way in terms of who goes to jail. And the criminal justice system serves to keep a certain class of people under control. I am assigned to defend people accused of rape and I do it as well as I can. I'm not going to sell out someone's life, and for pay, because I happen to think he's guilty and that rape is a horrible crime. I would defend *anyone* to the best of my ability.

"I'd kill anyone who raped my wife or daughter."

John

He is a deputy D.A. in his mid-thirties who has tried some twenty rape cases, many involving battery, robbery, and homicide, and is highly successful at getting convictions.

I'd kill anyone who raped my wife or daughter. I'd find him and blow him away, I know I would. I'm very much aware of the inadequacies of the criminal justice system, and I'm sure I'd take matters into my own hands. It's like pulling teeth to get a guy convicted. You've got to give them their constitutional rights at every step of the proceeding, or else lose the conviction somewhere along the line. We've proven that he raped, robbed, and sodomized Mrs. So-and-so. But did we have the hearing in the proper amount of time? Did the police not abuse him when they questioned him? Did he get a jury of his peers? Did he have an effective lawyer to prevent his getting convicted? Did the D.A. commit misconduct in the course of the trial? Did he call him an animal for his attacks on this old lady? It's a joke. There's a million reasons why the case can be reversed. Liberal appellate courts wipe out conviction after conviction.

And cross-examination is very difficult for rape victims. It really burns me up sometimes. Say you have a really strong case where the guy breaks into a house, commits a burglary, rapes a woman, forces her to commit oral copulation; and say you have some beating of the woman, and there's fingerprints, or some other evidence which links the guy into it pretty strongly. You have a fairly cold case, and if you don't screw up jury selection, you're going to get a conviction. The defense lawyers know that; what the hell, it's a strong case and what have you got to lose? So if they can reduce the complaining witness, the female, to tears, or make her look bad or make her look stupid, they'll usually do it in a cold case. All they have to get is one person to hang up a jury, and then it has to go to trial again. It's never better the second time, *never* better.

Under the guise of legal advocacy for his client, a good defense lawyer will do anything he can to destroy the complaining witness. It really grates on me because it has nothing to do with the facts, it has to do with his attitude, but what can you do? Even if you object to a question and the judge sustains the objection, that very question may reduce your complaining witness to tears, or make her so rattled she's not going to recall the facts you've gone over—so you're dead.

How do you relate to rape victims?

They are obviously hurt by what happened. They don't like it, they don't like getting up there and baring the fact that some big dude has made them go through every imaginable little thrill thing. I just try to tell them: do the best that you can, remember everything you can, and *get even.*

A lot of the time when I talk to witnesses for the first time, I'm thinking about how I'm going to use what they say in my closing arguments. I could be busy jotting something down and not saying, "Here, cry into my handkerchief," and all that bullshit. I always think when I see the victim: What kind of juror is this person going to sell to? Am I going to keep twelve old ladies on the jury or do I need hardcore men?

To do a job like I do, you have to be coldly dispassionate, you really do. You have to size things up. You have to be thinking of what you're going to do from the first get-go. If the person isn't able to convince you of what happened, how are you going to be able to convince the jury?

D.A.s have been accused by feminists of being insensitive to rape victims.

I don't think you have to be overly concerned about what they think. They seem to figure that a cop or a D.A. is never going to have a bad day, never going to have a bad home life. You get so pissed off at the kids, and your blood pressure's 190 over 180, and you haven't had enough sleep because the baby's had you up half the night, and then somebody comes in and says, "You're not giving me the attention I deserve," and that all cops and D.A.s are like that. Sometimes victims have unreasonable expectations.

Women should realize that we're out to convict these bastards, and that rape victims should tell the whole truth to the police and the D.A.s from the start, or it could kill the whole case.

How do you "size up" a rape victim's credibility?

The major part's intangible. You have the police report in front of you, and you'll ask her to tell you the story again and you might notice something deviating from the police report. Then you'll ask her again. If somebody's lying, they're never going to get it straight every time. I don't care about minor discrepancies, but when you get into major stuff, that's when it matters. "You said this to the police and this to the guy on the beat and all of a sudden you're telling me something new." I quiz her on it and if her power of recall is off and she gets flustered, then it becomes a matter of intuition. You can just watch her reactions.

If she lies, for instance, about whether she goes a lot to a particular bar where she met the accused, and we check it out, then she becomes a real liability, because the defense is going to know it. So you've got a major discrepancy that you're stuck with on paper. And jury instructions are that if a person is willfully false in one material part of her testimony, you can distrust her whole testimony. I can understand how a woman might distort the truth when she tells her story to the police, but it's only going to make it harder to get a conviction.

How do you feel about dating rape or acquaintance rape? How do we adjudicate such cases?

If a woman goes to a singles' bar and she only wants to go so far, she better have some corroboration as far as I'm concerned before she says so-and-so raped me. You better have corroboration, because that's not like when somebody breaks into your apartment or picks you up at gunpoint.

To get to superior court for trial in most of our counties, a case goes through a careful screening process. What would you say, for example, if you're the charging district attorney down at municipal court and the police report comes in and it says, "So-and-so picked up so-and-so at a singles' bar, and they had dinner or went to her place, and he asked her if she's on the pill or has an IUD or whatever, and she says, "Oh, yeah." The guy feels pretty secure in that situation, and they have a few belts, and then the report says: "He raped me and spent the night." You're going to think something's phony; you're going to think, "Wait a minute, *come on.*" And it's easy to find out if some lady is on birth-control pills because you can subpoena her birth-control records. If she's willing to play—well, it's like the little boy who cries "wolf." Those are tough ones, they really are. I'm sure it does happen where it really is rape.

How would you legally distinguish those dating rapes that you would really want to call rapes from those you wouldn't?

Legally, there's no difference, especially if there's no corroboration and it's just her word against his.

Even your most hardcore feminist is going to be more offended if a child or nun gets raped, or if your home is invaded by an armed robber and he rapes you in your home. When you get into your social settings and dating situations your outrage is diminished by the preparation and the situation in which the woman has voluntarily placed herself. I don't know if that's going to be acceptable to a lot of feminists but, hey, life is life.

But we don't want to be saying, in effect, that just because a woman goes out on a date with a man, she has to have sex with him.

That's like the guy who takes a chick sailing and they're having a good time drinking wine and sailing, and the tide's going out at forty knots an hour and he says "Okay, take off your pants or get out." What's she going to do? What're you going to do? The situation looks like: "Well, I went sailing on the bay with him and we went downstairs and we got it on," when the truth of the matter is that you either get raped or drown. I could see that happening, and I'm sure it does happen, but you better have some corroboration for that to make it stand up in court.

How can you have corroboration in the situation you described?

I don't know. The law doesn't deal so much with bad judgment as it does with cold, hard facts. That's the best way I can put it. There are a lot of rapes that don't get reported because I'm sure the female knew that "God, what a dummy I was."

What do you think of the new laws that make it illegal for a man to rape his wife?

I wish they'd never even passed the law. The only time you're going to see it is when there's been a legal separation. I don't think you're going to see any convictions. I think you're going to see something like the case in Oregon where the guy got charged and they acquitted him, and two months later they're back together.

I don't like it at all. I think it was done as a concession to the feminists. I don't like it. I mean, God, you marry the guy, you've slept with him before. Where's the horror? Where's the shame of being raped? It's not like your sixteen-year-old virgin who gets taken off the street, or even goes to a disco and gets taken by some guy when she uses bad judgment. Where's the horror? Where's the shame? The guy has fathered your children. All of a sudden he rapes you. Now, sure, you can say it's my right to my own body, but the crime is diminished considerably.

Suppose you have a situation where a couple splits up, and they haven't seen each other in a while, and they're both seeing other people, and they're considering getting a divorce, when he breaks into her house and rapes her?

That's over and above the normal spousal rape cases. Most people have the idea of spousal rape where the wife says, "I have a headache," and the husband says "Tough shit! I want it now!" And so he forces himself on her. That's what the feminists would like to see charged. Well, that's life. How are you going to legislate against life? Let's face it, there are a lot of things that are unjust in this world. That's certainly among the lesser of the evils.

The criminal justice system just cannot take every one of those cases that come forward as far as I'm concerned. Everyone laughed in this office when the spousal rape law was passed. Conceptually it's really nice—our bodies are private and we've got the right to them, etc.—but the practicalities of it really stink. Feminists are talking from emotion rather than practicality. There are a lot of factors they're not considering.

We should go after the more serious crimes in all cases. There can be a burglary of an uninhabited dwelling. Technically, it's a burglary. We've got better things to do than waste our time on that.

What can we do to stop rape?

You're not going to stop rape. Social rapes are always going to happen. I don't care if it's Adam and Eve, or Luke Skywalker and Princess Leah, it's always going to happen. That's just human nature. I think you can make it very, very difficult in robbery and break-in type rapes. The penalties are getting very severe. The word's going to get out on violent rapes, and you're going to see the crimes go down.

"We still have older D.A.s in the office who have classical attitudes toward rape, like 'Where's the crime?' "

Robert

He is in his late thirties, a senior trial deputy in a D.A.'s office who has been involved in hundreds of rape cases in various capacities, and has prosecuted over thirty rape cases himself. A woman who counsels rape victims describes him as "the attorney most sympathetic to rape victims in the D.A.'s office."

Attorneys find rape hard to talk about and easy to joke about. There are two kinds of rape jokes I've heard attorneys tell in the D.A.'s office. One kind is probably very similar to what men in nonlegal positions probably tell, like "Oh, yeah, this case, what did she lose in being raped." Or humorous comments based upon evaluating a situation in which the victim was either somewhat sexually provocative before the rape occurred, or where the attorneys have some knowledge of her previous sexual behavior and basically they say "Where's the crime?" There used to be jokes made about black-on-black rape—the same thing: Where's the crime? But I haven't heard this in the last eight to ten years.

The other type of jokes that you get relate to legal situations. I heard about a situation in which a rape victim was very incensed waiting to meet the attorney who had the case at the preliminary hearing, and finally the secretary tells the attorney that the victim's waiting, and she comes into his office and he's reviewing the paperwork in this case that he's going to put on this afternoon, and then he starts laughing and smiling and goes next door and she overhears him telling another attorney, "Oh, yeah, this is the one where the gal said she could probably recognize his penis again, that it was longer than six inches," and he's joking about it, because of statements the victim made in response to questions from the police. The attorney must have known that the victim could hear him, and yet he talked about it next door.

There are also things like "Hey Joe, this is so-and-so" (introducing the victim). "She's the one who recognized the guy two weeks later down at housewives' market and called the police.

Remember that one? That was pretty good, huh?" These things reveal a lack of sensitivity to the rape victim herself.

When going into the victim's prior background was available as a tactic during preliminary hearings and trial, more of these jokes and comments were made. Attitudes are changing and sensitivity to victims is changing. Women's groups have been helpful in educating the society at large and that has affected attorneys. It tends to be fairly easy to educate most D.A.s about this. We still have older D.A.'s in the office who have classical attitudes towards rape like "Where's the crime?"

The comment was made at a meeting I was at last year, "We ought to look at some of these rape cases. You're sending some awfully thin cases up here to superior court. You realize the poor bastard is sitting down there in jail while these cases are winding their way up here to superior court!" Which is interesting because from the same person who said that, there was no sensitivity at all to anyone else who was wasting away in jail while their case was being sent up here.

To some degree there's a reaction against feminist groups by some of the older hard-liners because feminist groups make noises about how we mistreat rape cases. You'll get reactions simply because they're being attacked. They might say things like, "Oh, Christ, another rape case. Goddamn, if these women's groups weren't screaming at us, this case would never have been charged."

There is a resentment among some D.A.s against rape victims, particularly when the woman herself is not willing to fit into a fairly passive victim plot that we have for rape victims, but becomes more assertive and wants to be involved in sentencing, or doesn't want there to be any plea bargaining, or wants to be informed each time a new date is picked. So as rape victims become more assertive, there is a reaction against them among some attorneys.

Basically, we have a protective attitude toward rape victims, just like we would have for our wives and daughters, as long as it's a stranger rape, where the victim and the rapist didn't know each other, as long as it's clear who was the bad guy and who was the good guy. But when it's the grayer form of rape, the softer form where the man and woman knew each other before, that's when traditional attitudes reveal themselves.

What attitudes toward rape do these rape jokes reflect?

The central theme is the damaged property theme. It's never really expressed because it's pretty tough to justify openly. Again, unless it's a stranger-on-stranger rape, which then becomes our classical picture of rape, and which by the way also means the victim probably didn't do much to invite it, then the general attitudes we see in men and women appear, i.e., what did she lose? or she asked for it, or she contributed to it in some way.

The property can be virgin property or defended property. For a long time the laws said a woman had to resist physically, and if she didn't resist, it wasn't a rape. And even today in seventeen or eighteen states you have to resist or it's not a rape, even if a gun is held to your head. The attitude is: "You have something there which we have appointed you to defend, and you didn't do it. You didn't resist all the way, and because of that you got what you deserve." In California and in most other major states, if you don't resist because of fear of great and immediate bodily harm, then that's okay, but it has to be that special kind of fear.

One of the biggest problems that men who are related to rape victims have occurs when there's no resistance. I think that they would almost like to have scratches and cuts and bruises and bullet wounds. They would almost rather see that than hear, "I immediately lay down when he told me to lie down. When he told me to take off my clothes, I took off my clothes." I don't know if they always ask, but they will want to know: what did you do to resist?

Is that due to hurt ego and wounded pride?

Yes, I think so. It's as if they have some goods here and those goods are supposed to be defended. It's like the feeling a man has when his wife has had intercourse with someone else. It's the feeling that someone else has enjoyed you, you were mine and you are not mine anymore.

It's certainly a case of defended property when you're talking about fathers and daughters. We have numerous cases involving thirteen- to fifteen-year-old girls who are coming into a sexually active period, who are attracted to older men and who don't have a chance to be sexually active with boys their own age, and so they get involved with these older men, and some kind of consensual sexual contact occurs. It's different from father and daughter type incest, which usually is coerced. I'm talking about a consensual situation that is brought to the authorities when it breaks off. The girl gets too possessive or whatever, and then she goes to her mother or father or friends and eventually it gets to the police, and then we have a situation where father wants this case to go to the Supreme Court, and the death penalty is not enough. I'm sure a lot of this conduct occurs which never comes out. But once it does come out, she becomes father's property, which he has to protect, and the biggest problem we have if we don't go all the way for forty years in prison is with the father. He's at every court hearing, he's calling the D.A.'s office all the time, and what it boils down to is damaged property.

What are your feelings toward the rapists you prosecute? Do you ever hate them?

I can't think of a defendant I've hated, which includes some murder defendants. It would be awfully tough to get into that kind of feeling and be in this kind of job for very long. While it is an emotional job, you tend to flatten out your emotional response to what defendants do, if only to be able to live with it.

I have certainly despised or had serious contempt for defendants in the past. Phoning up rape victims and making threats, and not saying who you are on the phone in a situation where we wouldn't be able to trace the call, and then the rape victim calls us in hysterics, has really pissed me off. I normally do get pretty worked up either in cross-examination of a defendant or during final argument. I normally think that's the time to be emotional. So there's an outlet for my feelings.

In a sense, the area of feelings toward the defendant is a different ballpark. We aren't even in that ballpark. We're simply into the different legal games you play in order to see that the accused gets punished.

Who make the best jurors in rape cases?

Younger women and men are better jurors. Older women tend to be incredibly critical of rape victims. "Why didn't she do this? Why didn't she do that?" They really want to separate themselves from the victim. So they will go to great lengths to point out things they don't like. Women twenty-five or younger are in the middle of the attitudinal changes about rape and they will tend to feel more commensurate with the victim. If there's any hint at all of feminist attitudes, they are kept off the jury by defense attorneys.

There are a couple of types of men jurors. There's the fatherly type who basically wants to put his arm around the rape victim and hold her. If you have a clean stranger-on-stranger rape, they're good jurors.

Younger men of twenty to thirty tend to look at the accused and think "There but for the grace of God go I." And in a soft rape situation where the man and woman know each other beforehand, they are very difficult jurors. Basically they say "Hey, come on, if a gal gets that far, she wants it. They left the bar and went to his house, and she had a drink with him, and then he said they got on the bed and somewhere along the line she started protesting, and she said she only took off her clothes because she thought he was going to hurt her. Well, come on, you don't go to a guy's house late at night when you know what's going to happen, and if you go, that's too bad."

There are also some younger men who are attuned to feminist attitudes, and if you can find them and they can stay on your jury, they're great.

The rape victims I've spoken to who've reported their rapes and gone through the criminal justice system invariably say that they

*wouldn't want to go through the process again. How do you
respond to this?*

If you're saying it's a depressing situation, I think it probably
is. But I personally characterize the area as one of immense progress in the last few years, progress being a relative term. Though
there are classic examples daily of rape victims being mistreated,
I think that a rape victim has a much better go of it today than
she did five years ago.

I personally think rape victims deserve some counseling
before taking the stand. They have a right to know and be prepared for what they're getting into. It's quite possible that at
the end of the line, the rape victim gets damaged much more
than the rapist, in terms of what we do to her, what the system does to her, and in terms of what happens in the community.

Because of the failure of the criminal justice system to deal
with rape, if you can call it a failure, we're seeing a more violent
reaction on the part of women to rape. I saw a billboard with a
vodka ad that said, "What is an ice pick?" and apparently it's a
vodka drink with lemon juice and ice. Someone had spray painted
underneath it: "An answer to rape." In talking to feminists I find
an increasingly violent attitude toward rape, which is understandable. And we're going to see a more violent reaction to rape as long
as the perception exists that the system doesn't deal adequately
with rape cases.

"I try to be as ethical as I can while at the same time trying to
do the best job I can for my client."

Ken

He is a thirty-four-year-old public defender who is married to a feminist, and strongly supports the women's movement. At times, he finds himself in the position of defending rapists to the best of his ability, as he is bound to do, both by his personal ethics and the strictures of the bar association.

I always do the best I can for my client. When I get a case, I essentially have to dissociate myself from the morality of what someone may have done and focus on the legal issues. Sometimes a confession has to be suppressed, or the fruits of a search suppressed; sometimes I keep my clients from testifying and just argue the nonconvincing aspects of the prosecutor's case, even if I may know my client did it.

In your zeal to get the best deal possible for your client do you ever, in rape cases, appeal to the sexism of the jury?

Let me pinpoint different types of rape cases. There are the cases where the man jumps from the bushes with a knife, or crawls through a window at night, and overpowers a woman. In that case, no jury's going to be sympathetic to the rapist, even if the juror is sexist. In those cases, sexism will work to the woman's favor because she's on a pedestal. Look at the sentences now for rape—they're skyrocketing.

Another type of case where you *could* appeal to sexism is when the victim is a prostitute. This is a typical case where the D.A.s will make jokes and offer the guy a misdemeanor charge, even if the woman was beaten up.

I had a case in which an eighteen-year-old kid in high school picked up an attractive sixteen-year-old girl and offered her a ride to school. He drove her to a dead-end street and said, "Okay, let's get down," and she said, "No! No! Take me back to school!" And he took her back to school.

Somehow, this got up to felony court and he was charged

with attempted rape, although he only tried to lay her, was rebuffed, and drove her back to school. I argued that you can totally disagree with this guy, he's an asshole, he crudely attempted to have sex with this woman, but he didn't try to force her. I argued that if *this* is attempted rape then half the men in fraternities have attempted rape and our prisons should be filled.

There are cases where a woman is raped who was wearing provocative clothes—a miniskirt or no bra—and some attorneys will argue that she was asking for it; what man could resist; boys will be boys. They would argue the weakness of men, and that women are femme fatales. I can see somebody making that work. I can see an attorney consciously selecting a jury with the idea that these people will go for that and then appealing to those sentiments and getting an acquittal. I don't think I could argue that convincingly because I don't believe it. I'd know some jurors would be thinking it and the question is, would I leave sexist jurors on the jury? In a sense, it's my job to keep sexist jurors, just as the D.A. is trying to get feminists on the jury.

In a dating rape case where there's a consensual-type relationship up to a point, and where force was used, if I honestly believed there was a chance the woman was taunting the guy, was really being a prick-tease—and I realize that's a stereotype—I would argue that side of it: that it was not unusual for this guy to get angry and do what he did under the circumstances. I would argue that this is a sexist society in which men are brought up to treat women as objects of desire that they can dominate and treat as any other commodity, and that a woman who acts coy or flirts is engaging herself in socially conditioned behavior. I'd talk about my client, who's not a well-educated person, who probably had certain notions about what the evening was going to be about. He's a victimizer/victim of society. I'd try to show that he's not an autonomous person, that he's caught in this sexist configuration where he forced this woman to have sex either because he thought she owed it to him or he couldn't resist, because this sexual stereotype that she fell into was so overpowering for him that he couldn't control himself.

I may go so far as to say that what he did was wrong—all of us probably wouldn't do it that way, and sure, he's no great hero —but because of the interaction between them, and their cultural conditioning, his using force was somehow understandable. If the victim was very flip and casual on the stand I might say something like, "You saw her demeanor on the stand. She didn't appear extremely upset about the situation. Maybe she didn't particularly want to do it at the time, but you saw her demeanor." And I might argue that her flip, capricious manner might have led my client to believe she fits the old stereotype of the woman who really wants it but is saying no.

Isn't that just a sophisticated, sociological way of appealing to the classic rape-supporting myth that men can't control themselves in the presence of a sexy, provocative woman? Men have been saying for years that "if a woman is sexually provocative and gets raped, that's too bad," which I think is nonsense.

Now that you say it, I think you're right, I would be in the position of appealing to that stereotype. I try to be as ethical as I can while at the same time trying to do the best job I can for my client. I'm sure that by trying to do an objective social analysis of the problem, I'm justifying certain stereotypes and rationalizations that should be done away with in a utopian society. And the real problem is: a simple no should be enough for any man, no matter how much foreplay. It's always been enough for me.

How would your wife feel about your appeal to the jury? She's a feminist.

She'd hate it. She'd probably be outraged if she knew the cases I have. I don't even discuss them with her.

Postscript: Upon reading this interview, he wrote: "You have captured the contradictoriness (sophistry?) in the way we are forced to treat these cases, but that's what I said."

6

Doctors

"... some women invite rape by placing themselves in vulnerable situations."

Alfred A. Messer

He practices psychoanalysis and family therapy at Northside Hospital, Atlanta, Georgia. His latest book is entitled, When You Are Concerned with Homosexuality *(Abbey Press, 1981). He is fifty-eight.*

When we think about rape we have to consider many different motives. There's the man who knows a woman casually and asks her out. He feels very insecure in his role as a man and tries to interest her in some way in sex. But when she puts him off he drives to a vacant lot and rapes her. In his fantasy she will be so overtaken by his sexual prowess that the experience will lead to a permanent relationship. Nowadays we're also seeing the man who asserts power over women by victimizing them sexually. What is readily apparent is the anger involved in this aggressive act. Sometimes he might even force the woman to stimulate him, as a further act of submission on her part. Then there's the psychotic we read about—the man who dismembers his victims afterward. Recently on television there was a story of a woman who was raped when a gang of intruders robbed her home. On their way out they became interested in her because there hadn't been much to steal. They forced her to submit sexually to all four of them as revenge for not being richer.

What I want to focus on here, though, is something that isn't talked about: there are women who do invite rape. It's not mentioned in polite circles, but for reasons of guilt or mystery or doubt, some women invite rape by placing themselves in vulnerable situations. As an analyst I hear many fantasies from women, and now, increasingly from men, who fantasize about being raped. The idea is that if I'm being raped, I'm not in control, and I need not have any guilt about it.

You know the joke about the nun in San Francisco. A sailor comes back from leave after being on ship for a year and he says to his friends, "Goddamn it! I'm so hard up. I'm going to the port and the first woman that comes along, I'm sorry, she's it." So he gets off the boat, grabs the first woman who comes along, drags her into the bushes, rapes her three times, gets up and shakes himself, and says, "My god, it's a nun." So he tells her the story that he's been away for a year and so forth and he says, "Please, I feel so bad; let me go to the Mother Superior so you won't be punished," and she says, "Don't worry, I'll explain it to her. I'll tell her this guy grabbed me and raped me four times, if you're not too tired." Well, that's the joke. He raped her three times and then she said, "If you're not too tired, you'll rape me four times." Some women have rape fantasies like the nun. She couldn't help it if she got raped.

Morally and legally, it can be a very difficult situation. I testify in court frequently, and in rape cases it's tough to give an accurate assessment. When you listen with a clinical ear to the evidence, you can almost sense in some instances that the woman provoked the rape by her appearance and behavior. The man has to prove that he was provoked and seduced, but it's difficult because legally he's committed a crime. Sometimes the man will get friends of his to testify that they went out with the woman and she issued them invitations as well.

We have to look at the total picture. If the man has a history of previous rapes that's suggestive evidence—at least it's known that he's capable of it. Don't misunderstand me. I've treated a number of women who've been raped and it's a horrible violation from which the woman hardly ever recovers. But speaking as a clinician, there are some women who invite rape.

"Being invited to rape." You're almost assuming that men are helpless before a certain kind of "feminine wile."

Some men are. Women have the capacity to arouse a man— there's no question about that. And once the man gets involved, once the sexual motor gets going, the sexual drive may take over.

Today, if you go to a rape crisis center they'll tell you that rape is a power trip, an aggressive, violent crime. That's sometimes true but not always. It's almost un-American to say the other thing, that it has to do with sex. But unfortunately it has to do with sex in various ways. I do evaluations for the police: a year ago I saw a man who was twenty-two or twenty-three, who had very little confidence in himself—the guy who hangs around the filling station. He goes out with a girl whom he knows and he tries to get her drunk and tries to get her aroused, and if he fails to get her aroused he may rape her. If he can't entice her, his desire for sex is such that he'll rape her. In this case the rape is a product of sexual need and the motive is primarily sexual gratification.

It's part of the feminist movement to deny that a woman can be a sex object and that a man can try to seduce a woman for sex purposes. Twenty-five years ago when I started in training, rape was looked upon as a sex crime. I see it as a psychiatric symptom.

Feminists have argued that rape is an attempt on the part of all men to control all women, that rapists are doing the job for men at large, so to speak.

That *sounds* perfect, but it's a lot of bunk. There is some truth to the idea that women have been oppressed and have been made inferior, and so forth, and rape becomes a symbol for that. But I think rape is an individual crime and I don't think it has to do with the social situation per se.

People are amazed that in this period of great sexual liberation rape is increasing so astoundingly. You would think that right now men could go to a singles' bar and find a woman. You would think it would be the easiest thing in the world to find a sexual partner. So why is all the raping going on? We know that there is something in the social fabric to which we are responding. But I don't agree with the generalizations of Susan Brownmiller or Kate Millet. Yes, men have subjugated women, but there's a different reason for that.

In birth and growth and development the child feels very much under the power of the female. A man is socialized by a woman. A man is fed and nurtured by a woman. A man is denied the breast by a woman. So a man grows up with a certain anger toward a woman. The boy growing up is saying, "Well, goddamnit, I've got to get even. I can't allow myself to be defeated, can't allow myself to be subjugated." In families of lower socioeconomic status, not only does the woman have the power, but because of A.D.C. and other grants, once or twice a month is Mother's Day, when the woman gets her welfare check. Not only is she the power in terms of being the maternal figure, but she has the financial power as well. So you find a lot more brutalization of women in these families, because the woman not only has the emotional power and the nurturant power, but she has the financial power, too.

Could we infer from this that as women get more financial power, men will express more anger toward women?

It's a logical step. The fastest growing symptom in psychiatry is male impotence and there are a number of reasons for that. One is the competition that men have for women. Second is the idea that a man nowadays when he goes out with a woman wonders how she's going to judge him versus the last guy. That, incidentally, is the cause of a lot of homicide. A man goes out with a woman and she makes disparaging remarks about his sexual performance. A man who's teetering on the brink may kill her because that is such a terrible insult.

There's no question that the women's movement is resulting in a backlash among men. There's a principle here that you have to use—synergy—which means harmony. We developed the automobile and the automobile has given us marvelous locomotion. But the automobile has caused us pollution and traffic accidents and so on. The women's movement has been wonderful in many ways. I'm a women's liberationist from way back. When I was in training in the fifties we would see women who were "career patients." Their children were grown, their husbands were successful. They had nothing to do, so they'd develop symptoms and go from one doctor to another. The feminist movement has taken care of that; you don't find many career patients any more because they can go out and work. But part of the result of the feminist movement has been an increase in rape, an increase in impotence, and an increase in homosexuality. One reason there's more homosexuality today is that men feel more challenged by women to perform.

A terrible situation exists in most U.S. cities. Women are often afraid to walk at night. Women are often catcalled and harassed when walking by themselves. Very few men acknowledge this and some men even get pleasure out of the feeling of superiority it gives them.

The biological mandate is that women are helpless and dependent at one point in their lives: when they're pregnant. Who's to protect them? Men or other women? The custom has been that men are the protector. Because of this, certain customs have grown up—that I hold a door for a woman, and tip my hat to her. All of this mannerly behavior comes because we recognize that women are at a disadvantage at certain points in their lives, particularly when they're pregnant. A month or two ago, I was having lunch at a hospital; one of the female doctors took her tray and started to sit down beside me. I'm old-fashioned: I automatically jumped up and pulled her chair out. She sat down and said, "If you ever do that again, I'll crack your face in public!" I said, "Okay, okay. I'm sorry, forgive me." She really got my attention. Why did I stand and pull out her chair? I'm saying that I'm there to protect her.

If you want to think of the way we've been socialized, when a woman walks on a street by herself at night the idea is that she's fair game. She's unattached. She has no protector with her. The woman who is escorted is not fair game. The whistles and catcalls are basically a sexual thing, an attempt to excite the woman. It may not be pretty, and many women find it offensive, but you and I have seen many women who smile delightedly when people whistle at them.

But aren't men who do that trying to punish women?

I would accept that in the sense that the woman symbolizes mother. I think women resent it, but again, they have to take a deeper perspective. The deeper perspective is that we've built in certain family structures so that the women can be dependent when necessary. That is the way I look at it.

When the hostages came back from Iran and had a press conference, one of them, a Marine, said, "Hell, we're all right. Let me get out of here and get back to chasing girls." When he went back to Texas he was welcomed by girls with signs that read, "Sergeant so-and-so, chase me!" It's normal for Marines to chase women and whistle at them; this is just part of our culture.

We're derived in western society from the tradition of the hunter. Men have had to be socialized to be aggressive. Women haven't until now. When you ask me what's going to happen a few years down the road: according to the militant feminists we should have nonsexist toys and nonsexist this and nonsexist that. I don't go along with this. I think you have to teach the difference in social roles because you want to socialize women so that they can feel good about whatever they do. It troubles me when I meet a woman who says, with a pained expression, "I'm just a housewife." I say, "That's wonderful. I hope you're happy in that role. There's no need to be embarrassed. You might want to do something else in the future and you have that option. Right now you're giving your children the nurturing they need."

"If men weren't so overstimulated sexually, they'd find it much easier to relate to women as people."

Slava Ellis

He is a successful psychiatrist, acupuncturist, and an instructor in psychosomatic medicine at the University of California Health Sciences Department, where he teaches medical students a course on self-perception and its effects on physiology. Ellis is thirty-four, in his second marriage, and has an eleven-year-old daughter.

Some of de Sade's writings were sexually exciting to me when I was about eighteen. What was exciting to me was de Sade's ability to create a whole other world of sexual possibilities. He did all these weird, awful things to women with no qualms, no guilt. In *Justine* I remember thinking "I hope something nice happens to her," but it was one catastrophe after another. What's interesting about the fantasies I recall is that the woman is basically faceless. The power isn't over another creature but over another body. It relates to the whole omnipotent male attitude, the Pygmalion myth: the idea that I'll fuck her and she'll finally realize what life is all about. . . .

Previously, it wasn't necessary for men to relate to women intimately as people different from themselves, but now it is. It's hard to make a distinction between expressing your power and manipulation. There's an extreme form of manipulation where you're clearly manipulating someone, but there's a gray area that needs to encompass your understanding of the person you're relating to. The same behavior might be asserting your power to another man and manipulation to a woman. So a woman might feel manipulated when you didn't want or intend to manipulate.

Have you ever felt sympathetic to the common myths about rape, i.e., that women can't be raped, or that women who claimed to have been raped were really consenting?

I've never believed those myths. I felt sympathetic to them after encountering a fair number of men who felt that way, sympathetic in the sense that I could feel their frustration and denial and chaos, which comes from feeling that they've *had enough,* enough erotic stimulation. You could call it feeling "prick teased," which to a considerable degree is how men grow up. It's not often talked about. The exceptions in my adolescence tended to be either wimpy secluded scholar types who didn't seem to feel their sexuality much, or people who ran in the fast crowd who were getting sex.

My own experience of all this sexual stimulation was on the one hand feeling impotent, and on the other yearning for sexual experience and not knowing how to find it or whether I would be able to run the social risks involved. The necessity of being aggressively and suavely seductive took me five years to learn, and was something I resented because it really didn't get me what I wanted, which was tenderness and love and acceptance. Instead it intensified the degree to which I objectified women. My fantasy was that if you're forceful at just the right time, she'll give in and you'll get laid—the Hollywood paradigm. My experience was that if I were forceful, but not physical, I usually was able to seduce the woman, but if I became at all physical, which happened once or twice when my own urges got out of hand, the woman backed off really quickly, which frightened me. . . .

The issue to me is that men are imprinted much like ducks on certain forms, textures, skins, whatever sexual stimulation they grew up with. And for centuries the only power women have had is as sexual stimulation for men. Sexual stimuli trigger a whole sequence of emotions and behavior that are very hard to stop. And many women don't take responsibility for it because it's the only power they've had. It was communicated to them in a very ambivalent and charged way by their mothers and the culture that you don't really talk about your sexual power, but you use it. Women are in a bind: if they don't behave like sex objects they get punished for it, and if they do they dehumanize themselves. The women I know who are successful know how to say no in very clear definite ways in addition to being very proud of how they look.

If men weren't so overstimulated sexually, they'd find it much easier to relate to women as people. I'd like to see lawyers take on sexist advertising, which reinforces the idea that women are willing and ready.

The men I've known who've felt sympathetic to rapists feel as if a boil's ready to burst. Emotions and wants surge about inside that they can't articulate. Most men never learn to express what's inside them. In these men, the frustration stems from a thwarted need to be held and touched. And not getting what they want, their only recourse, given that all of America says you have to get laid to be a man, is to wind up feeling that the only way to treat a woman is to rape her.

The men I'm talking about would agree that taking another person's sexuality is not very different from taking their life. But they also feel that rape can be justified. The attitude is: "I'll kill anybody who raped my wife, but that broad walking down the street who's wiggling her ass too much deserves to be raped": the only way to quiet what's been stirred up is to rape her. . . .

The nearest analogue to rape for women that I'm aware of is the pre-Christian Greek Dionysian festivals which happened twice yearly in which women left their husbands and families and ran amok in the streets. Young goats were especially prized and women tore them apart with their hands and teeth, and in some festivals there are historical accounts of men being torn apart. It was a frenzy devoted to expressing the kind of frustration women must have felt at being treated as chattel. It comes out of the same kind of impotence men feel currently.

What do men have to gain by allowing rape to flourish?

What they have to gain is easy intimidation of their wives or the women they're with, keeping women "in their place," keeping them afraid to go out. Men know that they wouldn't mind walking out in the street and if they're with a woman there's not going to be any problem and it's tempting for them to even maybe giggle a bit about women being frightened, when all women have to do is carry a gun or go to karate class. But it's clearly not that simple. It's like being a hypocritical bully. . . .

Physical intimidation can be subtly implied. The expectation that a man can be driven crazy or berserk sexually is common. "Of course I have my civilized decency, but if you push me any further I'm going to go nuts." And that's physical intimidation. The male attitude is "I'm really a bully but not taking responsibility for it. I refuse to take responsibility for it beyond this point. If I smell your vaginal secretions, I will go crazy."

What men have to gain by ending rape is a little more long term, because men will be forced to find other ways of maintaining power, their own individual power, rather than their power en masse as men. Men need to confront their blindness. It's a negative incentive in the sense that you have to experience pain in order to grow. You have to experience your own powerlessness, your feminine side, your intolerance, your arrogance, and the deprivation you had to suffer by objectifying women. There's an initial ego loss involved in admitting these things. It's a first step.

Once that's out of the way you have the further pain of experiencing what you repressed and learning to show your feelings and take risks in the midst of a lot of fear. The incentive for going through this is being freer inside, having more control over your destiny and a wider and more intense gamut of emotions. And if you can feel your emotions better you're more likely to have a better orgasm, and more of a true sense of what you want.

There's no indication that many men are willing to go

through these processes. It's going to take generations for men to change. Capitalism, Madison Avenue, and most jobs create fierce competition and require objectification.

What has your experience in therapy been with women who've been raped?

Women invariably feel a great deal of chaos and rage and guilt after being raped. I try to focus on helping the woman express her outrage clearly.

Maybe half of the rape victims I've treated have been able to feel their rage and their powerlessness about being raped only after they stopped feeling guilty about the sexual sensations they experienced during the rape. For some women, if they feel anything sexual at all, it retroactively condemns them. Women I've spoken with felt condemned and betrayed by their bodies because they had sexual sensations when they were raped. It is understandable that a woman might experience sexual sensation, and in no way implies that she's masochistic or encouraged it. A common formulation is that if a woman experiences sexual sensations when raped, she either wanted it or she enjoys being punished.

What happens physiologically, in rape, is that because of the fear involved, there's a significant disconnection between the higher cortical centers and what's happening in the rest of your body, so that any mechanical stimulation in the vagina causes primitive centers in your spinal cord to respond, and they send information back through the spinal cord so you feel you're not completely anesthetized, but you don't have any control over the physiological events occurring in your vagina. So, although you don't have any control, you feel responsible, which is a crazy situation to be in.

The rape victim is in a terrible dilemma. She can resist physically and create spasms in the walls of the pelvis and risk physical harm, or she can relax physically and run the risk of experiencing sexual sensations and scarring herself psychically. I'd advise women to relax and experience whatever sexual sensations might arise. The point is that this isn't all you experience. The dominant experience is some massive kind of alienation and fear, a very minor aspect of which might be the sexual sensations, but a woman recalling those sexual sensations will be in a lot of pain in this culture. Either way she tries to deal with the rapist she's bound to get hurt, which is the nature of the crime. . . .

Women quite reasonably don't want to address the subject of sexual sensation in rape victims because many men will try to exploit it, specifically by saying, "Ha, ha, you wanted it all along."

It might be easier to address the issue if the sexual sensations rape victims feel is seen not as giving aid to the enemy, but rather in terms of an understandable physiological response, thereby realizing that women are *not* responsible for whatever sexual sensations arise, and in fact they have been conditioned by men to feel responsible for something they *can't* be responsible for, which is one of the reasons rape flourishes. Women's not admitting the bind men put them in by raping them makes it all that easier for men to rape them. It may keep rape victims from reporting to the police or talking about it to people they feel close to. . . .

There are also a lot of women who don't get caught in this bind and they're the ones who are able to talk more freely about what in fact happened to them, and feel just outraged rather than chaotic about having had sexual sensations. That should be the main object of work on rape: to help women feel their outrage rather than feeling responsible and chaotic.

The subject should be opened up and men should learn to talk about it. From my own experience, men are very frightened of talking about rape. . . .

I have never spoken to male psychiatrists about their ideas, fantasies, or feelings about rape, and I spent three years in psychiatric residency in a good hospital in Boston in the early seventies. Men are afraid to address their feelings and fantasies about rape, afraid they'll uncover something in themselves, because they want to deny the possibility of having rape feelings. The classic explanation is that if you're really terrified to talk about something like this, the eventual analysis is that you also want it very much, so it's possible men are afraid to talk about rape because it turns them on, but I'm only speculating.

How does Hollywood support rape?

There's the classic movie scene in which the hero kisses the heroine against her will, and a struggle ensues, and he's overwhelming her and there's always one moment which is underscored, in which her resistance and struggle turn to moaning and heavy breathing and surrender.

The message for women is: pleasure will make you powerless. As soon as you start having sexual sensations, you will be powerless.

The message for men is: you can inflict pleasure on a woman against her will. This message appeals enormously to frustrated men.

What are the psychodynamics of rapists?

I think rapists probably destroy their feminine sides, what Jung called the anima. The destruction of the man's anima comes in all the different, probably multifarious, steps you need to go through in objectifying the woman to the point of being able to rape her. The man denies his feminine side so that he is unable to identify with the woman. The woman becomes the other, the unrecognizable, the one that needs to be vanquished, the prize that will assuage your own pain. I think rape proceeds initially from pain and then rage, to action. In order to prevent rape, you need to feel your sadness but you can't feel your sadness because that'll make you feel less of a man. In fact, if you feel the sadness you feel refreshed and much better able to deal with what the issues are afterward. So there's a flagrant lie going on. What is the function of that lie? When I've lied to myself about my sadness, it was to keep me from feeling vulnerable, as if it would turn me into a woman with all the negative connotations of being weak, being used, being unable to move. The social pressures against a man showing his sadness are real.

The very act of lying about your sadness and having to repress it accentuates your rage. If you feel your sadness and go through it you can still feel indignant and mad at somebody who hurt you, but you won't want to kill them or rape them. Rapists are unable to feel sadness in a way that relieves them. Anything feminine in themselves is very threatening. You would have to be out of touch with the feminine self to develop that degree of distance and objectification in order to rape. Rapists need to overcome the feminine and subjugate it and make sure that it stays down, and the final blow is the rape itself. . . .

Is there any truth to the notion that a man can be provoked by a woman's appearance and lose control of himself?

Well, men obviously have a choice on the basis of their feelings. You can feel whatever you want, but if you hurt someone because of it that's completely different.

I really don't think it's possible that the way a woman acts or dresses could in fact mechanistically elicit a complex sequence of behavioral events. It's impossible. It might be more difficult for some men to control themselves if the basal level of certain brain chemicals is different, but that's still speculation and hasn't been shown.

If you're opposed to sexism in advertising are you also opposed to pornography?

The double side of the dilemma is that women grow up at least unconsciously realizing that the way they look gives them a tremendous amount of power. To give up sexism in advertising women have to confront giving up that power as a manipulation and I don't think women are at all willing to do that today. The lesbian contingent certainly is, and maybe one in ten nonlesbians would.

Most women are unwilling to condemn sexist advertising because they don't want to confront the whole issue of how powerful their sexuality can be. If they confront that then they're going to be terrified. A large part of the terror of rape is not knowing your own power.

"Re-raping the victim happens a lot in emergency rooms."

Herb

He has been an emergency room doctor in a big city for eight years and has treated hundreds of women shortly after they were raped. He is in his late thirties.

Re-raping the victim happens a lot in emergency rooms. The most important thing medically in examining someone who's been sexually assaulted is not to re-rape the victim. A cardinal rule of medicine is: Above all do no harm. That's a negative focus and I'm not completely comfortable saying that. But in my experience in the last eight years, I have been singularly impressed with how vulnerable and sensitive victims are to all sorts of intervention by various people. Rape victims often experience an intense feeling of helplessness or loss of control. If you just look schematically at what a doctor does to the victim very shortly after the assault with a minimal degree of very passive consent: A stranger makes a very quick intimate contact and inserts an instrument into the vagina with very little control or decision-making on the part of the victim; that is a symbolic setup for a psychological re-rape.

So when I do an examination I spend a lot of time preparing the victim; every step along the way I try to give back control to the victim. I might say, "We would like to do this and how we do it is your decision," and provide a large amount of information, much of which I'm sure is never processed; but it still comes across as concern on our part. I try to make the victim an active participant to the fullest extent possible. Even though that is the goal, the reality of the situation even under the best of circumstances is a negative one for the victim.

There's a principle of crisis intervention called primacy, which says that people who intervene early after any crisis situation have enormous impact on the victim. That can be very good and very bad. It happened more in the past, but I'm sure it still happens a lot these days, where a physician or a nurse or a forensic pathologist does a relatively insensitive examination soon after a sexual assault and compounds the emotional trauma that occurred. So I try to rely on the positive side of the primacy phenomenon. One common criticism I hear is: "You're a male and you're doing the examination. Don't you think it would be better if a woman did it?" For a long time that made me very defensive. Since then it has occurred to me that a male figure who is trying to be sensitive and considerate to a rape victim very shortly after she's had an interaction with a male who's been very insensitive and inconsiderate, can potentially correct a lot of damage.

You're talking about the reestablishment of trust. You have this enormous power over a woman shortly after she's been raped to influence how she's going to relate to men in the future.

That's a point that's very difficult to get across to staff a lot of times. They'll say you're babying this person or taking yourself too seriously. But again I think back over the last eight years and it is really phenomenal to me how exquisitely sensitive to nuances of mood and behavior and verbal comment rape victims are. Something you say to someone in a crisis situation can be totally misinterpreted or interpreted in a totally different way from something you would say to a friend over coffee.

Most abuses of rape victims are not due to any conscious malevolence on the part of medical personnel. An emergency room is a high stress area to begin with; there's a large flow of patients and in-depth counseling isn't given to anyone except under the best of circumstances. For self-protective reasons, medical personnel tend not to delve into the area of emotional trauma. They tend to be rushed, which tends to make the victim feel that she's not very important, that the doctor is trying to get the examination over with because he doesn't want to do it. That confirms feelings of worthlessness, dirtiness, and guilt.

Doctors often assume an objective pose for reasons of self-preservation, and that may be the doctor's motivation for appearing cold and detached and disinterested. The victim may take that to mean, "He doesn't really believe I was raped," when that's not the doctor's attitude at all.

Another important way in which medical personnel do damage to rape victims is through implicit attitudes toward sexual assault that they have as members of our culture. Doctors may try intellectually to control these attitudes but they've been programmed to have them. Once again it's a situation where the attitude would not be picked up except by a vulnerable, suggestible victim. I'm talking about the myths that a woman is raped because she wants to be raped, and if she wanted to prevent it, she could've; that she shouldn't have been in the park at night because everybody knows it's a dangerous place; that she only did this to get back at her boyfriend. Hundreds of reasons that I see as attempts on society's part to deny the seriousness of sexual assault.

Some rape victims report doctors saying things like: "Now we're going to see if you really were raped," just before beginning the examination, as if they're only worth taking seriously if they're physically torn up.

That attitude has been very prevalent in our society and I'm sure in the medical profession for a long time. Here at the emergency room it's part of the training program to point out that the majority of sexual assault victims do not have serious injuries. Doctors are encouraged to look for very subtle injuries, which frequently are present, to corroborate the story of the victim.

Your specific example seems really insensitive to me and I'm sure it occurs many, many times throughout the country. Doctors often have very little training in how to treat sexual assault. I had absolutely no exposure to it in medical school. I started as an emergency room physician eight years ago, having never examined a sexual assault victim, and having, quite frankly, never given much consideration to the issue of rape, which was totally and effectively denied in my mind till I graduated from medical school.

What can emergency room doctors do in a positive sense in treating rape victims?

I would not underestimate the value of empathy. Empathizing with and validating the victim's confusion and fear and anger says to them that they're being taken seriously, and an enormous amount of trust and self-esteem can be created for the victim. That's an important part of the recovery process. A lot of times policemen and doctors and other authority figures do not support the person's sense of worth and her self-esteem will suffer for a long time.

Correcting stereotypes about sexual assault that occur in the victim herself is important. For example, a woman is jogging in the park and the rapist jumps her and drags her into the bushes and sexually assaults her; she comes to the emergency room with an overriding feeling of guilt—"I should have known better than to go jogging in the park," or "I shouldn't have gone out alone." Those are myths and we try to correct the myths. We say the park is there for you to jog in. It's not there for people to get raped. People are frequently raped at home; people can be raped when they're not alone. The only reason you were raped is because you were available and you were considered to be vulnerable by the person who happened to be there. There is nothing you did wrong.

Another common example is a woman who is confronted with a rapist who has a gun and goes along with what happens to her in a very passive sort of way, and afterward says, "I should have done something, I might have gotten out of it." We very strongly support the fact that she did do something: she went along with it in order to retain her life. That's particularly important these days with a lot of emphasis on self-defense. A lot of women feel that they should've fought back and that can at times be dangerous. It's important to make the victim aware that if she is still alive, then whatever decision-making process she went through was the right one.

So just being sensitive and empathetic isn't enough. Not to confront those myths is to support them.

You have to become active yourself and correct the distortion as it occurs, but it's also a myth in our culture that in this sort of situation you can simply say that you shouldn't feel guilty and take care of it. It's necessary to recognize that the rape victim may continue to feel guilty for a substantial period of time, and part of your crisis intervention may involve simply allowing the person to ventilate feelings that you feel to be inappropriate.

There is an enormous amount of work to be done with sexual assault victims, who have only been legitimized really in the last ten years in the medical literature. Enormous strides have been made in the case of rape victims, due largely to the efforts of very militant feminist groups who have demanded that law enforcement and the medical profession take a good hard look at themselves and recognize that the work they were doing in the past was pretty lousy.

"I don't like to baby them too much, either."

Lou

He is twenty-nine, has worked as an emergency room physician for six months, and is considering making a career of it.

In treating rape victims, I stay with the medical aspects of rape and avoid the psychiatric side of it. That's more comfortable for me and I was trained that way. When the victim comes in you have to take a history and ask them involved questions, and that's real uncomfortable sometimes, depending on the patient. Some patients are able to project a real calm image and that, in turn, makes the physician calmer about taking down the history. Other people get very emotional and that's the hardest part of dealing with the rape victim. But most of the people I see are pretty well composed. They might be crying a little or maybe sobbing; I've only seen a few really hysterical people.

When people get real emotional and on the verge of hysteria, I tend to shut them out and get very professional and just get what's needed on the form. I don't have very much patience for that. Some doctors do, but I don't. You see people coming in here in emotional and physical pain, and you get calloused after awhile.

Do you feel at all uncomfortable about medically examining a woman's vagina shortly after she's been raped?

I don't feel uncomfortable physically examining them. You just have to be a little more aware that their body has been violated, so you have to be a little more gentle and more understanding than in a regular pelvic examination. When you do pelvic exams you have to be concerned about the patient and understand that it's kind of a precarious position to be spread out on a table with your legs up in the air. If you just respect them for that, it goes pretty easy. I don't like to baby them too much, either.

Would you be more sympathetic toward a rape victim who was physically wounded than one who wasn't?

Yes, I think so. You tend to think, "Well, maybe she was consenting." I know a woman can be raped and have no abrasions or lacerations. Sure they can be raped, but you tend to be more sympathetic toward someone who has physical injuries that you can see.

7
Policemen

"I let them know that the questions will be embarrassing, but that they're necessary."

Art

He is twenty-six and a sergeant on the city police force in a university town in the Deep South.

We had a case a year and a half ago where a woman was in the shower and when she stepped out, a guy threw a towel in her face and raped her. When I was walking her out to my car to take her to the hospital, she was laying her head down and finally started crying and asked me, "How does a woman live after this?"

She wanted me to tell her. I said something to the effect that, "Life's gotta go on. You just go on. You try to put it behind you. Nothing like this will probably ever happen to you again. I know it's hard for you to believe that and understand that, but you can't live in constant fear." You just talk to her and give her moral support and tell her how people won't consider her bad.

Do you consider it your responsibility as a policeman to comfort her?

I don't know whether it's my responsibility as a policeman but I know it is as a person. As a policeman you've got to be compassionate to an extent and you've gotta be objective and you've gotta be able to put your foot down. You can let things go so far and then you've got to stop them. I've become a lot colder person as a policeman to where death doesn't bother me anymore, unless it's with kids. I've got two kids of my own. That's the only thing that still gets me. That still has an effect on me.

Cops are generally harder core people. You have to be or you'd go crazy. We cut jokes. You see a guy with his eyeballs hanging out and you just detach yourself from the situation. You have to. The other day a girl killed herself and I said, "Hell, she ought to be ashamed, she made a mess for us and look at what it's done to her family. Hell, no, I don't feel sorry for her." And in a way, you don't. In another way you feel, "If somebody could've helped her . . ." If you spent time feeling sorry for people you'd lose some of that objectivity. One of my favorite sayings is "Que será, será." You do what you can do but after that you don't worry about it. A lot of things you don't have any control over.

How do you relate to women shortly after they've been raped?

I probably have more sympathy than most police officers. My captain on the last case mentioned something about how well I can relate to the women. I just let them know right off that I can't fully understand what they're going through, that I do have a very good idea but there's no way that I could actually know because I'm not a woman; and they come across to me pretty well. I let them know that the questions will be embarrassing, but that they're necessary. I let them know what they'll be going through. We take them to the hospital and explain to them what the doctor is going to do. That's usually the biggest thing for the woman. Usually she's scared and nervous about going to the hospital. She doesn't trust anybody, she feels like she's been violated. She's ashamed, she feels dirty, she doesn't want anybody looking at her and that's one of the big humps that you've got to get over. Some doctors you have problems with. They might grin. I have that problem, I smile too much really. That can be misinterpreted for a doctor. If I was standing there with my clothes off and somebody walked in and grinned, it would send waves of embarrassment through me. Rape victims are very sensitive. They know what's going on.

How do you determine which cases should be prosecuted?
We had a case reported this morning. She said she'd been raped by about four guys that she knew. They'd all been out together drinking and had gotten just sloppy drunk. She said they took her clothes off and beat her and raped her. She did have a busted lip. She went to sleep, she said, after they raped her, and slept for two or three hours and decided to call us. With that kind of situation, well, you know what they say about a woman that travels around. She says she woke up and her clothes were off—that's just not going to get it.

In cases where the man and woman knew each other, you just have to feel it out. If it's a dating situation and she says, "Well, I let him undress me and then I changed my mind," when it gets to that point you decide, "Well, you can hang it up." But the woman who goes out on a date and she asks him to take her home and he refuses and drives out on a dirt road or something, that one you can understand for sure. The girl just didn't know the guy that well and that's the kind of guy we'd charge.

If the woman's been living with the guy for two or three years and he rapes her, we generally talk to them and they decide against pressing charges. You try to explain the situation to them, what they'll go through in court and help them look at it realistically and let them know that they don't stand a chance. If they're living together and the guy beat her up and knocked her out and raped her, then she'd have a chance. If the guy said, "Damnit, I own you, I'm going to beat your tail and kick you out of the house," and the woman decides to submit and lay there and let him have his fun, then she'd have a very tough time with that and there'd be no point in going to court. I've had enough cases in front of juries so I can just about tell which way it's going to go, so why waste time with something? Why lie to them? All I can say is, "I know how you feel but this is the way it is. You've got to accept it." I try to tell them in a nice way.

I'm not going to lie to a woman and tell her she's got a case when she hasn't. She'll devote all her time and energy into putting this guy away and it'll be bearing on her mind and then the defense attorney tears her apart and the jury brings back a "not guilty" verdict. Then in addition to being raped she's got the problem that nobody believes her. Why give anybody false hopes? I call 'em like I see 'em. . . .

In cases where the woman doesn't know the guy then it's a real challenge to find him. It's like a small fire that spreads and then pretty soon it burns itself out. You'll look for the guy, you'll work at it, trying to find all the clues to get him off the streets; you worry about other women and if you haven't caught him in a couple of weeks, you've got so many new things coming in that it just goes to the back of your mind and you can't put much effort into it anymore.

Is the way a woman's dressed when attacked a significant factor in deciding whether to prosecute?

If she's dressed provocatively it doesn't help. When she comes to court, the D.A. tells her to wear a nice homely looking outfit—a long dress with a high neck, high-heeled shoes and little makeup. Most jurors will go by that; they want to know how much provocation took place. There's a problem if you've got the defense attorney saying she was walking down the street with a slit up to her tail, wearing no bra with a see-through blouse. Jurors are going to be influenced by that.

I really don't believe that women bring it on themselves. A co-ed walking on campus at three o'clock in the morning is not taking the necessary precautions, but she's not bringing it on herself. A lot of college-age guys out at that time will have been drinking and you could have the kind of rape where a guy's not out for domination like most rapists but wants a little bit and sees it's convenient and decides to take a chance on it. That would be an extreme case where she didn't bring it on herself but she should've taken more precaution. It's still rape and it doesn't influence me personally, but it would a lot of your jurors.

If a guy can't control himself he needs to be taken off the

street. Some rapists may look at any attractive woman and think, "Well, this is the last little bit I can stand. That does it." In my opinion, the way a woman's dressed isn't that much of a factor. If he's not morally sound enough to resist it, he doesn't belong walking around. It's a way of laying the blame on someone else. It's like a guy who runs out on his wife and says, "I got drunk and couldn't help it." He knows what he's doing.

What do you think of marital rape laws?

It would depend upon the amount of force used. If the woman just didn't want to and the guy jumps her and she submits because he's stronger, that would be hard to prosecute. I've been married a little over nine years; I got married when I was sixteen and I would never force it like that on her. I can't fully realize what some of the families go through. I see it every day—the woman that's scared to leave or feels like she can't leave or worries about her children and how she's going to feed them if she leaves. We go to family fights week after week; you go to the same houses, you talk to them, you explain to them about divorce and counseling and then you get tired of going back to them. They hit each other over the head with sticks and rocks and shout at each other and stab each other, and then you ask why they don't separate and they say, "Because we love each other."

I feel like that would be a problem we'd run into if we had marital rape laws. Plus the number of cases that would come in where it would not actually be what you would consider a rape. It would be partly forced, but it wouldn't be so much forced as it would be submission on the wife's part. There are other resources; they can get out of the marriage. If you had a marital rape law that specified that it would apply only in cases of separation, you could hang them on that.

What would you do if your wife were raped?

I would very likely try to stay calm in her presence and not show the hatred I would feel for him. I've had times where I go to sleep worried about her and wake up with a nightmare. One day she was out back in her bathing suit and I went to sleep and I guess that triggered it. I thought about her being raped. I dreamed that I got up and looked out my window and saw this guy on top of her and reached up and blew his brains out. That is really the hostility that I'd feel toward him. To the wife, your mother, any close family, you want to rip 'em apart.

A guy kicked my sister's door down one time and she was scared to death. She was screaming, crying, about to fall to pieces and we caught the guy and I said a few words to him. I was shaking and when I start shaking that means my fuse has grown very short. I consider myself pretty cool, calm, and I don't lose it too often. I made a few promises that if I caught him around there again, if I caught him harassing her, that I would have to throw him in jail and that I would hope he would resist. That was as far as I could go. I couldn't say, "I'd like to kick your ass" or anything like that.

If I hadn't been in uniform, I can't say what I would've done. I could very well have carried through with what I had dreamed. A guy who does something like that I have no use for. The same with kids. A child molester is to me the lowest scum you can have. Above that would be your rapists.

"If you took it, say you took it."

Al

He is in his mid-thirties and has worked as a sex crimes investigator for five years in a large southern city.

I don't think you can ever say a woman invites rape, because a man does not *have* to rape. A woman may become a likely target for rape by the way she acts. But even if a woman's walking down the street nude at midnight, that still doesn't give anybody the right to rape her. A lot of policemen take the attitude that she invited it. I just don't believe that a woman wants to be raped, because she can go out and give it away. Why be raped when you can go out and say, "Come have sex with me," and there are a lot of guys that would.

What would you want to know if your son were accused of rape?

Whether he did it against her will. If he did it against her will, that's rape. That's all that matters. I told him, "If you go out and take it, they'll lock you up. Don't call me and don't lie to me about it. If you took it, say you took it." A lot of times guys will come in here and say, "I didn't take it, she gave it to me," or some old story. It really insults my intelligence because I grew up in the streets, too; I know what those guys do because I've seen it done, I've had friends do it. My best friend was accused of rape and he did it. He'd been doing it ever since we were little. I know this city and some of the cats that hang out here and I wouldn't put anything past them.

I think if men can get away with it, they'll just go out and take it. It's all a matter of self-restraint. I see a lot of good-looking women out in the street. I'm not just going to go out and grab one and take it. That makes me less than a man if I have to do that. I feel that I should be able to talk a woman into it. If I can't talk a woman into it, I don't need it. There's always another day. If she won't give it to you, somebody else probably will.

Most people have a conception of rape that a guy goes out and just grabs a woman off the street and beats her half to death and rapes her. Most of the rapes don't happen like that. A lot of times, she may know him. She may meet him at a bar and they ride home together. She may invite him in at three o'clock in the morning. It still doesn't say that she's got to have sex with him because she invites him in. She may just want to talk. When I was growing up, you never did have sex with them on the first date. The second date you might not have sex with them. In fact when

I was in college I went with a girl a whole month before she would let me have sex with her and she had screwed almost every guy on campus. Just because a woman invites you up doesn't mean she gives you consent to rape. People around here believe that because she takes you into her home, you've got to have sex with her. If she tells you she does not want to do it, that is rape and that's the law; until they change it I'm going to lock 'em up.

Do you get emotionally involved in cases?

Not really. It's just a job. When I started at this job five years ago I was all gung ho and I wanted to lock up everybody. By now I've seen every kind of rape that could possibly happen and I don't get emotionally into it. Either I find the guy or I don't find the guy. But I do my best to find him if I can. If you got emotionally involved you probably wouldn't get any convictions because you couldn't be objective.

A victim complained that I didn't seem compassionate to her. I told her why I didn't. It's a job. I told her I can't sit here holding your hand. You're not the only case I'm working on. I said, "You got raped today. I got four or five more that I'm working on that happened last week. I've got some more that'll happen today or tomorrow." I say, "I just have to work yours like I work everybody else's. I can't show special attention to you."

I guess I show a little compassion because I'll talk to her, you know, and I won't holler at her and scream at her and tell her that she should've done this or she shouldn't have done that the way some people do. I'll listen to her tell her story and then I'll investigate it, and then if I find out she's lying I'll tell her I just don't believe her or I don't think we can prosecute. I have to admit we've had a lot come through here that tell lies on the guy. Some of them come in here and tell me they were raped by a guy they've had sex with before. Once they tell me they've had sex with the guy before, there's almost never a prosecution. And if they were boyfriend and girlfriend, the jury will not find 'em guilty unless he beats her half to death.

What would you do if a man raped your wife?

I'd kill him and I wouldn't even report it. I'd just find out who he is and I'd kill him. Nobody would ever know but me.

"There are times, we joke, that the rape occurred *after* the sexual intercourse."

Jack

In his mid-fifties, he has been a policeman for twenty-five years and a sex crimes investigator for six.

Most rape victims are very honest and frightened, and many of them have extended fears and apprehensions. The person who's frequently most shook up and difficult to deal with is the boyfriend. They are extremely emotional and defensive. I have one now that I'm working with who can't understand why the rapist isn't instantly caught. Everything possible has been done; there are no clues and the girl can't identify him. Boyfriends are frequently very angry and want to kill the guy. In their overly protective attitude, they are creating a problem. Frequently, the woman is made more upset because of the problems in their relationship.

A very lovely young lady was raped very violently and humiliatingly in front of her apartment house, and she was honestly and seriously upset. The boyfriend she was living with thought she was overexaggerating the seriousness of what happened, and insisted that she have sex with him. Technically, he raped her as vigorously as the suspect. Psychologically and physically she was not ready, and he demanded it and she gave in, for whatever reason.

He raped her as forcibly as the guy who did before. He just held her down and took it. Now how does that man justify that? Some men give women a very low status in their lives. . . .

In talking to rape victims, you have to find out exactly what happened. Sometimes they're reluctant to talk; sometimes you can't shut 'em up. Motive is always a point. Generally speaking, I believe something happened, I believe what the lady is saying happened to her. But I'm also aware that someone else looking at the incident may see it a little differently, and that's what the jury's going to be doing—examining the whole picture. There are times, we joke, that the rape occurred *after* the sexual intercourse. The cases where people meet, and she'll come into his motel room and they go to bed; the fellow's a little impatient and when he gets done with her, he says, "Bitch, get out of here!" That's when the rape occurred, not during the intercourse. If he'd been nice to her afterward, she probably wouldn't have reported the rape. She's hurt, there's a scuffle, she gets slapped—all the components of a rape are there. It's difficult to sort all this out.

To her, she was raped and she's very sincere about it; she didn't want to go in there, she admits she was wrong in going in to the guy's house or apartment or motel room. She shouldn't have had a couple of drinks with the guy, but she got raped. Probably, when she had sex, it was in the gray area between consent and coercion. I advocate a misdemeanor rape law. All the do-gooders are saying every rapist should go to prison. That's not right; there's a lot of in-between in these things.

For instance, I had a case the other day where the ex-boyfriend came over and another guy was in the house. They have had intercourse half a dozen times, she says; he says fifty times. The other fellow in the house leaves and she says the guy slaps her and rapes her. *He* says, "The other guy leaves and we start socializing and hugging and kissing and we go into the other room and I tell her I didn't like the other guy being in the house. Every time I come over there's someone else in the house. We get into an argument and a scuffle and I slap her and she hollers rape."

Some guys are explosive and want it now. She probably

would've rejected him one more time if he'd played the game. Her medical report indicates that she probably did have forcible sexual intercourse. There's abrasions in the vaginal area and she's got a slight swelling in her cheek, so apparently there was some force used. I think she's been wronged; it's all compatible, she made a prompt report. Now should that guy go to prison or should he go free? I think somewhere in between. I think the guy should be held responsible for his actions, but I don't think he should go to prison.

Those types of cases aren't unusual, maybe ten percent. You'll see it when somebody accepts a ride in a car or with a prostitute. They'll get dumped out without their clothes in an isolated area, and say, "I've been raped." The sex has been agreed upon and conducted with enthusiasm, but they'll holler rape and you have to be quite careful. Frequently, someone in an automobile will say, "Come on, I'll give you a ride, little girl," and he'll demand sex. Even after he's taken it, if he's got a little class she probably won't complain if he doesn't push her around. It's the degree of force; a little discretion afterward is as important as before sometimes. She'll go along with it once. She may be raped, but often how the man treats her afterward determines whether she makes a report. If he apologizes afterward that may make a difference.

Are policemen sometimes insensitive to rape victims?

Absolutely. We work hard to train our police officers to be sensitive but I'm sure not all of them are as sensitive as they could or should be. It is a problem and we're well aware of it, but it's a matter of changing personalities and ideas that go back generations, and it isn't going to be done easily. Some officers are immature and nervous and unable to handle a situation with any class. Some people have class, some people haven't. Some of our officers at twenty-four or twenty-five haven't got any class yet.

Recently I was out with a very experienced investigator and we were at a rape victim's workplace. We had some pictures and the man said he wanted her to identify the man who *raped* her.

He said it loud enough so that other people could hear it; she may not have told the other people at work about it. It was obviously making her uncomfortable. Here's a man who's taught other officers not to do things like that. It made me wonder if sometimes I do things I shouldn't.

What's the worst part of being raped for a woman?

The fear. Most of them are afraid for their lives and feel that they're going to die. That's the only way they're going to give it up.

Some of the emotional trauma that we're led to believe always occurs, doesn't always occur. My observation is that women who have emotional problems after being raped had them before. They've not been stable. The rape may trigger off emotional problems but it doesn't start from there.

What should women do to keep from being raped?

It depends upon the circumstances. Usually the rape doesn't start when the rapist grabs a girl. If he jumps from the bushes and sticks a knife to your throat, your choices are few. If he comes up and he says, "Give me a dollar," the rape's starting right there. If she's fearful and submits and gives him the dollar, he's going to say, "Well, give me your wallet." If he takes her wallet, he's going to take her purse, and by the time he's taken her purse, he's going to take her body. It's a progressive thing. So the rape doesn't start when he touches her; it's the first approach. So a woman has to be continually alert that men are after her body. Some may take three months to get to the point, and some will take three minutes or three seconds, but that's the name of the boy/girl game. The boys want to get in bed with the girls.

Women have to be afraid and be alert. One way of looking at it is to imagine that you've just withdrawn $5,000 in cash from your savings account and you're going to deposit it in another bank. So you've got $5,000 dollars in your purse. How would you act differently? How would you park your car? If somebody were to approach you, would you act friendly or standoffish? If women were to act that way, there'd be a lot less rapes.

Some women get angry about having to constrict their lives.

Women and men like to trust and be trusted. Rapes have been going on for a long time, they're going to be going on for a long time—as long as there are boys and girls. There's a lot of strange people out there and boys are different from girls. I don't see any cure for it.

My job is secure.

8

An Advocate for Rape Victims Responds

"The underlying assumption in these interviews is that if somehow *women* would change their behavior, men might stop raping."

Andrea Rechtin

If attitudes toward rape are to change, we must have a clear sense of what attitudes exist. The foregoing interviews have been presented to reveal some prevalent attitudes. But to present a variety of male perspectives on rape, so many of which are misguided, without at the same time presenting an informed woman's perspective on the men, would also be misguided. Andrea Rechtin offers this perspective. She is sexual assault counselor/advocate for the Alameda County Victim Assistance Program, District Attorney's Office, Oakland, California. She has provided services to over four thousand sexual assault victims in the past five years. She is an advocate for victims in the courts, refers most of the victims she sees to therapists, and helps victims obtain compensation for wage loss, therapy, and other medical expenses. She provides training and education on sexual assault in the community. She is twenty-eight.

After reading these interviews, I wonder whether we have learned anything in the past few years about why men rape. It took me days to figure out why I became so incensed. It was not that men view rape that much differently than women, because unfortunately too many women see rape *exactly* as these men do. But what these men would have us believe is that rape is not a crime of violence but is instead some extreme form of sexual seduction; and that in some way, women are to be blamed for being raped because we provoke sexual hostility from men. The underlying assumption in these interviews is that if somehow *women* would change their behavior, men might stop raping. I guess in the past five years of working with rape victims I've been wanting to believe that attitudes are changing, that we as a society are beginning to understand that rape is a violent crime. What makes me so angry and what even scares me is that I see these interviews as a step backward in rape education. It's clear to me that so many of these men have spent a considerable amount of time, perhaps even years, becoming "sensitive" to rape but their convoluted "raps" have never been challenged or questioned critically either by themselves or by others. I hope that other people reading these interviews will realize that underneath all their rationalizations these men still believe that rape is seduction, no matter how brutal the crime.

How should *rape be viewed?*

Let me first give you an example of the double standard we set only for sexual assault victims. Compare rape with armed robbery. Armed robbery is no less a crime if the victim is uninjured. As a matter of fact, bank employees are taught to remain calm and are rewarded if only the money is taken. It's a real double standard in rape because if you don't fight back, you're blamed for not protecting something everyone tells you you're supposed to protect, because rape is seen as a sexual crime. None of these men talk about rape as a crime of violence which is inflicted on persons, female *or* male, of *all* ages. They do not talk about rape as a form of violence, primarily against females, whether that violence is beating your wife or mother or molesting your own child. They never discuss rape as a violent crime among many other crimes. Most rapes occur along with other crimes— robbery, burglary, assault, kidnap, attempted murder, or even murder. We must realize that rape is always a crime of violence, even if the woman is not beaten. Rape is *not* seduction and we are never going to understand rape if we view it as sexual behavior— rape is a hostile and cruel act of violence which threatens the life of the victim.

Why is it important for us to look at rape as violence?
While looking at women's behavior and discussing sexual tensions and role relationships make it easier for men (and many women) to talk about the problem of rape, it will not help us to understand the crime, which *is* one of violence. The fact is, all of us undoubtedly have sexual tensions, but this does not explain why certain men rape women, children, and other men. To look at rape, we need to look at violence in our culture and the causes of that violence.

Women are being raped every day by men who are total strangers. Women are being raped every day by men whom they trust, whom they love, whom they may have known for years. It is easy for many of us to judge the victims involved and demand that victims change their behavior. It is far more difficult for us to confront our own anger about violence that rape brings into our lives or the lives of those close to us. When loved ones or women close to us are raped we are angry and fearful at having to admit we live in a violent community. We will also feel angry that we were unable to prevent that violence from happening. Violence breeds violence and it is terrifying for many of us to recognize that violence within ourselves. To accept rape as a crime of violence is equally terrifying.

The men interviewed, especially the therapists and psychiatrists, are not acknowledging that they have these feelings deep down. After all, labeling rape as a "psychiatric symptom" gives these professionals a fairly simple explanation. They see rape only in terms of the psychological stresses of certain situations triggering the sexual impulses over which rapists have little control. This thinking subtly shifts responsibility for the crime back to the victim and allows the professional to distance himself from his own feelings of anger about violence. These professionals would have us believe that rape is not really a crime of violence but only a sexual aberration on the part of rapists which is brought on by some action of the victim. It makes the crime easy to dismiss. It keeps your own life safe from the horror of the crime.

Some men I interviewed spoke freely of their rape fantasies. What does this tell you about the causes of rape?

Many of these men have the attitude of "yes, I *do* acknowledge my fantasies but I would never act them out. I'm not a rapist-type person." The premise is that it is the acting out of the fantasies that distinguishes a rapist from the rest of men in society. This attitude promotes sympathy once again for the rapist—that some provocation has unconsciously pushed him over some thin boundary from fantasizing about rape to committing the act. These men also want us to believe that sexual manipulation by women has confused and blurred the line between seduction and rape. Such confusion then makes it more difficult for rapists to know whether they are even committing a rape or not. I do not believe that rape fantasies tell us why certain men rape in certain situations and why others do not. Most if not all of us have sexual fantasies, but most of us do not rape others. Whether expanding our knowledge of rape fantasies will improve our knowledge of sexual tensions is questionable. I strongly believe that rape fantasies are not the cause of the crime. Instead we should look at why some men need personal violence and choose rape as an outlet.

You say men should be more self-critical of their feelings about rape as a crime. Why is this important?

The men interviewed rarely talk about their own reactions to rape. For those with wives or girl friends as victims, their reactions to rape dealt mostly with how their lovers responded during or after the rape and whether their relationship was terminated as a result of the rape. The men seemed capable of only two reactions to rapists: a passive empathy for the assailant who is somehow sexually provoked and/or a blind rage in which they want only to kill the rapist. The men feel this rage only if the rape is inflicted on someone close to them. The men see rapists as either perverted criminals or as ordinary men like themselves who were trapped into rape and are not criminals. They are uncomfortable with the reality that most rapists are otherwise normal men who succumb to criminal violence against women. Equally hard for these men to face is that rape is always a crime. When confronted with the facts of a situation these men will rarely deny that a rape has occurred but will typically argue that under the circumstances the act was not a crime. The Vietnam war vets, for example [see Chapter 2, A Variety of Men, "Daniel" and Chapter 4, Husbands, Lovers, and Friends, "Gary"], describe rape of Vietnamese women as somehow different from rape in the U.S. They say that you have to see rape in the larger context of American attitudes toward Vietnamese women, who were seen as stupid, to be killed if you wanted to, that they weren't human. That's *exactly* what happens when a rapist rapes a woman in America. One man [see "Daniel"] says the Vietnamese women became objects of fear and dread and that it was easy to feel angry at them. That's exactly what the "All-American" rapist [see Chapter 3, Rapist, "Chuck"] says, that it was easy to feel that kind of hatred toward women when he raped. Another man [see Chapter 2, A Variety of Men, "Mark"] fantasized about raping female Nazi guards. His rationale for doing that, he says, is to righteously punish them for what they had done to others.

It is important for men to begin to question how they feel about rapists if they are going to dispel their myths about rape as an extreme form of seduction. It is especially difficult for men to accept the mentality and actions of a rapist for what they are. A rapist is punishing a woman for what he believes she or someone else has done to him. Typically, the rapist will say to his victim. "I'm going to degrade you, show you who's boss; I've got power over you and you better accept it, bitch, because that's the way it is." How can this be mistaken for seduction? Rape is brought on by a rapist's need to commit personal violence and feel the power it creates, and not by the pressures of seduction fantasies.

Would you expand more on how you see rapists?

Rapists are not passionate. During the crime, they become cold, ruthless, and violent. The women become faceless objects. Women walk into court to testify and rapists will turn around to watch them. Some have even said "Oh, *that* one." What rapists tell women who they rape is that they feel degraded, angry, and inferior. They've been raised to feel superior to women and to other men. When a rapist feels put down, he tries to become superior again by raping an inferior human being, whether that be a woman, child, or another male. The rapist uses females primarily as a convenient target for his rage, not his sexual frustrations.

And it makes no difference if you know the man beforehand. Most of the men in these interviews don't take acquaintance rape seriously; it's somehow only really rape if someone breaks into your house and beats you. As one of the investigators said, "If only the man would be nice to her afterward she wouldn't report it." There is usually a Dr. Jekyll/Mr. Hyde personality to the rapists. In nearly every rape case I've seen, the man has apologized to the woman after raping her. He may give her a glass of water after breaking in her house and raping her in bed, he may drop her off at her house after kidnapping her, he may send her flowers two days later, he may call her up and ask her out for a date. I even had a case where the man said during the rape, "I really hope I'm not messing you up, I really hope I'm not because I know what it does to women, I know what it's done to the other women I've raped and I don't want it to happen to you." However, during the rape he was also telling her what a whore she was; he hog-tied, raped, and robbed her, and stole her car.

Typically rapists constitute a cross-section of society. They do not stand out as degenerates or sexual deviants. Many rapists are physically attractive, employed, have wives and/or girl friends, a normal sex life, and children. They wear nice clothes to court (sometimes suits and ties) and their family usually appears at court to support them. Most of these same men have long criminal records which include assault, robbery, burglary, and occasionally murder. A few rapists have long records for sexual assault only. A few men have a long history of sexual assault with no prior arrests. There is no typical rapist or typical rape situation. The common factor in rape situations is premeditated violence, whether the victim is a stranger or an acquaintance. A rapist may wait on the street for a woman to walk by or a rapist may ask a woman out on a date and "set her up" to be raped by himself and his friends.

I disagree with the interviewees who say we should view rapists as victims of their sexual fantasies. Many of the men interviewed obviously feel sympathy for the rapist's plight, of seeing the rapist being suddenly overwhelmed by a woman's provocative behavior and wanting her sexually no matter what the cost. Rapists are not out-of-control sex maniacs. They are calculating, deliberate, and dangerous.

What do women go through when they are raped?

Rape injures the core of your being. You can be robbed and beaten but being raped violates something very primitive and basic to your psychic being. You grow up believing that you have the right not to be violated. The fear is that you are not going to live through it, that this man will never let you go. The experience of being raped has little if anything to do with sex. Your mind is going fifty directions at once. How am I going to deal with this man? How am I going to calm him down? Do I fight? Do I submit and promise to do anything if he'll let me go? What's going through your mind is that your life is in danger. You're going to be raped and you may be killed. So if you can get out of it alive any way you can, by God you're going to do it.

What rape does is destroy for a woman her concept of what the world is—everything is turned upside down and demands reexamination before she can go on with her life. Rape can destroy your ability to respect and trust others, to be independent and

learn self-confidence, to see yourself in the future as someone other
than a victim. You question your intuition and your ability to
judge another's intentions and motivations. You question whether
you will ever feel safe again. You may live in terror for years
believing the rapist will return or that you will be victimized again
by someone else. You may isolate yourself emotionally, deny your
terror, become immobilized. You question whether the future
holds anything positive for you—you blame yourself for your own
victimization. You feel angry, sad, confused. You also feel that
"they" told me it was going to happen and "they" were right. You
start taking responsibility for the rape and ask yourself how you
could have prevented it. And what's worse, you have to deal not
only with your own emotions but with everyone else's around you.
Rape is one of those crimes about which everyone has something
to say.

*How are rape victims forced to respond to other people's
emotions?*

Immediately after you've been raped, you are incredibly vulnerable to other people's reactions. That's why sensitive police
officers are *so* vital to a woman's emotional well-being after the
crime. Here you've gone through this hellish ordeal, thanking God
that you are alive, and the last thing you need is someone question-
ing you about your motive for reporting or asking you questions
about your personal life or why you didn't resist more. If you're
hysterical, people think you're crazy or psychotic; if you're withdrawn and speaking in a monotone, people wonder why you're not
more upset. No one, not even yourself, realizes that you are in
shock, sometimes for weeks later. Victims, however, are acutely
aware of other people's reactions. Do they believe me? Who
should I tell? How will my family react? Will my father, my
boyfriend, my brother want to kill the rapist? What will they think
of *me?* Will they treat me differently? Will they blame me?

Rape victims are put in a terrible bind. Men expect women
to remain innocent yet women are blamed if they're not constantly
on the lookout. Rape victims are blamed if they do anything that

men call stupid or bad judgment. You are blamed if you are angry after the rape—anger disturbs other people and they are uncomfortable if you become hostile and bitter and resentful. You are expected to be forgiving and become your "old self" again, which of course is impossible. You're blamed if you don't talk to others about the rape; you're blamed if you talk too much about it and take "too long" to "get over it." You're blamed if you want to escape everyone associated with the aftermath of the crime and just go off somewhere else by yourself. If your boyfriend wants to kill the rapist, you have to calm him down. You probably won't tell your family because you don't want to deal with your father's anger and your mother's tears, because then you'll have to tell them everything is fine even when it's not and you feel like you're cracking inside. And so you internalize all your emotions in order to cope and people tell you how wonderfully you're doing and how proud of you they are. And deep down they wonder about the rape and feel rejected and angry because you shut them out.

People do not understand that being raped is not just "bad sex" but is violence inflicted upon your mind as well as your body and that it can affect your life for years. Many police investigators say, "I went out and saw her and showed her some mug shots. She's okay, she's back to normal. You don't need to bother her." And only months later, she's tried to commit suicide or she's gotten a divorce. For over half of the three thousand victims with relationships that I've seen, the rape precipitated a breakup within a year. Many of the remaining relationships break up within two to four years after the crime. Persons who are raped are of both sexes, all ages, all races, all socioeconomic groups. And each rape victim responds a bit differently to the assault depending on her upbringing, the way she has dealt with tragic incidents in the past, and the amount of support she receives from people close to her after the rape.

Why do you think violence is so threatening for people to think about? Why are there such strong reactions to rape?

Violence is threatening because we *want* to believe we have control of our lives at all times. Somehow if we take precautions then rape should not happen to us. Men are the ones who are given permission in our society to be violent and women are raised to be passive. Threats to your security are something women have from day one. You grow up female *knowing* that your life is inhibited and restrained in many ways because of the violence men can inflict upon you. But the anger doesn't tend to come out until after you've been attacked and you realize how truly vulnerable you are. It's difficult for both men and women to realize that no matter how many restraints women impose on their own lives, rape cannot be totally prevented. It is the irrationality and randomness of rape which is so terrifying deep down for us. So we find ways to blame the victim.

I was raped during my first week at a women's college. I was at a coed orientation dorm party. I had only dated one other person in my life before. The graduate school of the nearby college had been invited to the dorm. We were all sitting around and this graduate student invited me out for a walk around campus. We were walking along talking and all of a sudden he throws me in the bushes and starts pulling off my clothes. I never reported the rape. I *knew* it was my fault even if I couldn't figure out exactly why. Sometime later a woman was raped in the dorm adjacent to mine. I never heard anything else about it except rumors that she had left the college. When I was young I was also molested by my next-door neighbor. He was a "friend of the family." I always felt that was my fault, too, and never told anyone until recently. He always told me what a bad girl I was.

It is also terrifying to realize how prevalent rape is. Sometimes I wish that for one day I could believe that everybody in the world wasn't violent and that I could walk down the street and not have to look over my shoulder. I take a dance class. Of the sixteen women in the class, there are now five who I know have been raped in the last five years. I don't know about the others. The statistics say that one in four women will be sexually abused by the age of eighteen. Now it's being confirmed in my own life. Most women I talk to have been previously sexually abused. It may not be rape; it may be child molestation or incest or attempted rape. And it doesn't just happen to you once, it happens three or four times. I think most men have no idea what it feels like to grow up in that kind of reality.

You work in the courts. How do you feel about the way the courts see rape? How do you feel about what the lawyers and police say in these interviews?

Even though rape is a felony, as are other crimes of violence, and is legally prosecuted as The People vs. The Rapist, a crime against one's community and state, the courts do not view rape as a societal crime. They personalize the crime. This explains the police officers and D.A.s who react so emotionally to the sixteen-year-old virgin and who want to put their arm around her and tell her they will get that son of a bitch for her. The cases that are prosecuted vigorously are those where the D.A. is personally outraged by the crime. The D.A.s have a protective attitude toward the rape victim, just like they have toward their wives and daughters [see Chapter 5, Lawyers, "Robert"]. This attitude, however, also explains the reaction of the courts when the system fails in some way to protect the victim or convict the rapist. The blame is immediately shifted back to the victim—she wasn't credible enough, the facts weren't good enough, the victim had unreasonable expectations—instead of a failure of the court system. The courts see rape as a crime against the individual, not against their community.

Like others in society, police and lawyers and judges want to see rapists as different from themselves. It is far easier to see rapists as different from themselves. It is far easier to see rapists as sexual aberrants than as otherwise normal people who *choose* rape as the outlet for their violent feelings. The courts tend to deal harshly only with repeat offenders or those who severely beat the women during the rape. There is an underlying sympathy for the rapist who only threatens violence, rapes, and then apologizes profusely to the victim. It is difficult for people to believe that it is *precisely* that *threat* of violence, whether actualized or not, that is so terrifying and life-threatening to the victim.

Rape is epidemic in my county. Only one in ten reported rapists is ever prosecuted and only one in fifty is sent to state prison. Rape is on the increase in our society and more women are reporting it. What is happening, though, is that the more rape is reported, the more society wants to ignore it, and the more rationalizations the courts will find for blaming the victim, rationalizations that will deny the prevalence of violence. The incidence of rape is so high that the justice system is unable and/or unwilling to contain it. The professionals in the justice system are angry at their own inadequacies to combat the increase. They are also angered by our indifference to the crime; most people do not want to hear about the pervasiveness of rape.

These frustrations make justice system professionals angry and defensive. Their personal views of rapists are ambiguous and confused. They view rapists as either victims of sexual entrapment themselves or as incorrigible sexual deviants who should be incarcerated for life. What society tells our justice system is equally confusing. We pass laws for stiffer penalties for rape and determinate (fixed) sentences for all crimes of violence. At the same time, we tell our justice system professionals to incarcerate fewer criminals because the prisons are full and imprisonment has failed to rehabilitate rapists.

It is clear to me that all the recent emphasis on sensitivity training for police and lawyers will not solve the problem of the lack of prosecution and punishment of rapists. That became clear to me through these interviews. They epitomize for me what can be so damaging about rape sensitivity training as a solution to the problem of rape—professionals can *appear* sensitive to others by what they say, but underneath they have not changed their ideas or become self-critical in any way. It's all well and good to have persons in the system who in one hour or one week learn the sensitivity "rap" for rape victims but this will not help them deal with their own attitudes toward the rapist and crime he has committed. More importantly, sensitivity training does not say to the professional that rape is a crime against society instead of only against an individual. The rationalization in the courts is that as long as you treat the rape victim well, you are doing your job.

Unfortunately, while the rape victim may feel better emotionally while going through the system, sensitivity training does not in any way ensure that the case will be prosecuted vigorously. As long as our society and our court system, as a mirror of that society, continue to see rape as sexual conflict between two individuals, then we will never understand the proper role of the courts: to enforce the idea that rape is a crime against society, regardless of circumstance.

Do you have any general thoughts about the interviews as a whole?

Yes, I do. After many hours of thinking over these interviews and feeling such total anger at what is said in them, my view of them is that they are written for men but directed at women. By that I mean that they almost constitute an "I'm okay, you're okay" manual for rapists, male professionals, lovers, and friends. The interviews help men identify with other men about their attitudes on women and their attitudes on rape in a noncritical, nonjudgmental manner. The interviews are directed at women because the moral of these interviews is that *once again* women need to change their behavior, not men, and that rape will decrease as a result. By reading the interviews we, as women, are supposed to learn about men's anger at women and forgive their hostility and frustrations. There is no recognition by these men that rape epitomizes all violent crime where there is *no* respect for the value of another human life. As long as we view rape as seduction, and at worst unwanted sex, we will never understand rape. If we push ourselves to see the violence in rape for what it is, perhaps then we can begin to understand the degradation of rape victims. Rape is a crime which degrades us all and not just another form of aggressive sexual behavior between individuals, as these interviews would have us believe. We do not need yet another elaborate apology for violence, but the resolve to end our tolerance of it.

Conclusion

A woman, having been harassed by men, protested: "Why are they *so angry?*"

It will take much thought as yet unthought, by men in states of perception as yet unattained, to answer her. And any answer must serve primarily to assure women's safety. At this point in history men have only begun to acknowledge their anger at women, to reflect on its origins, to confront its manifestations. This book is, in part, an exploration of that anger, an attempt to give it air and light. In a culture where women are brutalized, where few men acknowledge that brutalization and fewer still evince indignation over it, just getting men to talk (more or less) honestly about rape has value. If a major attempt is to be made to confront the problem of rape, many things must happen. I will mention a few.

First, rape (and violence against women generally) must be perceived, pure and simple, as a *man's problem* and one that results directly from the way men regard women in American culture. Since 1971, when women first made of rape a contemporary political issue, women have agitated, educated, lobbied, learned self defense, formed rape crisis centers, rewritten archaic rape laws, provided better treatment for rape survivors, and given each other strength, confidence, comfort, and love. But what of the response of men? It is men who rape and men who collectively have the power to end rape. The enormous resources of American men—intellectual, economic, political—must be marshaled to that end. This will only begin to happen when men cease blaming women for rape. The many insidious and cruel maneuvers by which this is done—treating rape as natural, relating a woman's appearance to a weapon, regarding women as commodities, projecting sexual desire onto women, treating rape survivors as dupes, distrusting women's credibility, and generally imputing motives alien to women's intentions—must be clearly confronted.

Second, rape must be comprehended both in terms of the crime itself and the effect of its threat on women's lives. The ways in which the threat of rape alters the meaning and feel of the night and nature, inhibits the freedom of the eye, hurts women economically, undercuts women's independence, destroys solitude, and restricts expressiveness must be acknowledged as part of the crime.

Third, rape must be seen as part of a continuum of acts of violence against women which together constitute a major mental health issue for all women in American culture. Starting at the less severe end of the continuum such acts might include: harassment —rude stares and noises accompanying women as they walk down the street, grabbing or touching women's bodies without permission, unwanted attentions and intrusions, and suggested rewards for sexual favors in work situations; obscene phone calls; exhibitionism; Peeping Toms; spouse battering; dating rape, marital rape, and rape by strangers; incest; and femicide, the murder of women because they're women.

Fourth, marital rape must be given its full acknowledgment as a crime; laws must be passed in the forty states where it is currently legal.

And finally, a conversation must begin between men and women. Perhaps for a long time, the most urgent part of that conversation will consist of men listening to women describe their sufferings. In the past, most men have not listened. It is painful but necessary to acknowledge the sense in which men benefit from violence against women. Men compete with women in myriad ways, both professional and personal; the threats to women give men definite advantages. It is sometimes said that men tolerate violence against women *because* they benefit from it. This is doubtless true of some men. But few men seem to *consciously* tolerate it because they perceive benefits. And it is only from a competitive or antagonistic view of women that men can ultimately claim benefits. For men who care about women or (finally) themselves, violence against women benefits no one. It mystifies and poisons relations between men and women and vitiates the potential for trust, love, and surrender. I am convinced there are many men who, if they were to listen to women, would awaken to the reality of violence against women and take action. And "action" can range from contributing to a rape crisis center to joining an anti-rape group to talking to one's son.

How much longer will men accept as normal lives of constraint and abuse for women? I don't know. American men have an opportunity to reverse a part of history as old as history itself. History can happen fast. We must see that it happens soon.

Appendix: Men Against Rape

To repeat: Rape is a *man's* problem. It is men who rape and men who collectively have the power to end rape. The following men's organizations concern themselves with (among other things) issues of male violence against women.

California

East Bay Men's Center
2700 Bancroft Way
Berkeley, CA 94704
(415) 845-4823

Everyman's Center
c/o Humboldt Open Door
Clinic
P.O. Box 367
Arcata, CA 95521
(707) 822-3822

Los Angeles Men's Collective
2611 4th Street, Apt. B
Santa Monica, CA 90405
(213) 396-3655

M.O.V.E.
3004 16th St.

San Francisco, CA 94103
(415) 626-6683

San Diego Men's Anti-Sexist
Network
c/o Harry Brod
9242-B Regents Road
La Jolla, CA 92037
(714) 452-7544

Sonoma County Men's
Support Network
P.O. Box 4688
Santa Rosa, CA
(707) 542-5042; 526-1359

Colorado
Amend (Abusive Men

Exploring New Directions)
c/o Commission on
Community Relations
144 W. Colfax Avenue,
Room 302
Annex 111
Denver, CO 80202
(303) 575-3171

Denver/Boulder Men Against
Sexism
c/o Ken Yale
1435 Adams
Denver, CO 80206

Illinois
Human Resources Association
Foundation, Inc.
P.O. Box 5022, Station A
Champaign, IL 61820

Men's Program Unit
University YMCA
1001 South Wright Street
Champaign, IL 61820
(217) 337-1517

Kansas
Lawrence Men's Coalition
1100 Tennessee
Lawrence, KS 66044
(913) 843-6395

Massachusetts
Emerge: A Men's Counseling
Service on Domestic Violence
25 Huntington Avenue
Boston, MA 02116
(617) 267-7690

Missouri
Kansas City Men's Project
Westport Allen Center
706 W. 42nd Street
Dansas City, MO 64111
(816) 753-3844

RAVEN (Rape and Violence
End Now)
P.O. Box 24159
St. Louis, MO 63190

RAVEN is attempting to form a communications network of men working on issues of violence against women. They are putting out a newsletter called "Network News." Subscriptions are $20 individuals; $30 groups.

New York
Men Against Rape and
Sexism

c/o Bob Love
770 Elm Street Ext.
Ithaca, NY 14850

Rochester Men's Network
c/o Vocations for Social
Change
725 Monroe Avenue
(The Genessee Coop)
Rochester, NY 14607

Ohio
Cincinnati Men's Network
3618 Middleton Avenue
Cincinnati, OH 45220

Pennsylvania
Pittsburgh Men's Collective
5512 Bartlett Street
Pittsburgh, PA 15217

Washington
Seattle Men Against Rape
1425 E. Prospect No. 1

Seattle, WA 98112
(206) 325-1945

Wisconsin
Men's Place: Men Working
Together to End Violence
Against Women
P. O. Box 1582
Madison, WI 53701
(608) 251-7646

British Columbia
Vancouver Men Against Rape

c/o Michael Linehan
Box 65306, Station F
Vancouver, B.C.
Canada
(604) 876-0600

In addition to the above men's organizations I would like to mention the National Clearinghouse on Marital Rape (Laura X, Director). The Clearinghouse maintains seven hundred files containing a variety of information related to marital rape. Tax-deductible memberships are $30 groups; $15 employed persons; $10 activists, students, and unemployed. For more information send a self-addressed, stamped envelope to NCOMR, Women's History Research Center, 2325 Oak Street, Berkeley, CA 94708.

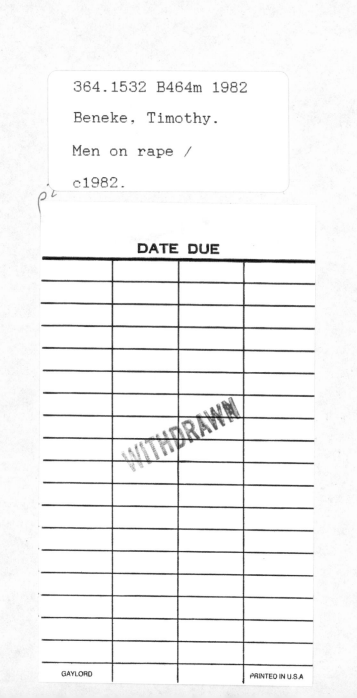